CHILDREN ARE THE REVOLUTION DAY CARE IN CUBA

BY MARVIN LEINER

WITH ROBERT UBELL

A RICHARD SEAVER BOOK

THE VIKING PRESS   NEW YORK

To Anne, Kenny, Karen, and Danny

*"We work for children because children know how to love,
because children are the hope of the world."*

—JOSÉ MARTÍ

A Richard Seaver Book ★ The Viking Press
First published in 1974 by The Viking Press, Inc.
625 Madison Avenue, New York, N.Y. 10022
Published simultaneously in Canada by
The Macmillan Company of Canada Limited
SBN 670-21629-1
Library of Congress catalog card number: 72-9740
Printed in U.S.A.

Acknowledgment
Grune & Stratton, Inc.: The chart on page 123
from *Disadvantaged Children* by Herbert Birch.
Used by permission of Grune & Stratton, Inc.

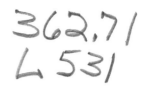

CONTENTS

When I first decided to examine Cuban education since the Revolution, it was my intention to study the entire system, from day care through adult education (which the Cubans call "worker–peasant education"). Miles of tapes, mountains of notes, and boxes of slides later, it became apparent that my initial report would have to confine itself to only one aspect of Cuban education. For a number of reasons, including the fact that early education is so important, and the subject of increasing interest throughout the world, I made up my mind to concentrate on day care in Cuba.

For a year during 1968 and 1969, my family and I lived in Cuba. My three children were enrolled in Cuban schools: my younger son Danny, who was seven at the time, attended elementary school; Karen, whose diary is excerpted in this report, went to junior high school; and my older son Kenny was a high school student. During that year I traveled the length and breadth of the island, visiting day-care centers and schools; observing classrooms in action; interviewing students, teachers, and administrators; taping, taking notes and photographs, and, wherever possible, gathering educational materials. Two years later, in 1971, I returned to observe more recent developments, which I report on in my final chapter, "Cuban Day Care Revisited."

My debts are many, and inevitably I may neglect to mention some of those who so generously gave me of their time and energy; if so, I am sure they will as generously forgive me. Special thanks are due to the following:

The late René Vallejo of the Revolutionary Government, who arranged my initial visit. His warm welcome, patience, and humor made those hectic first days much easier;

Abel Prieto Morales, who took the time on both my visits to answer endless questions about educational goals and practices in present-day Cuba;

José Aguilera Maceiras, who helped me understand the structure and methods of Cuban schools;

Orlando Ajuria, who helped me gain access to a wide range of both urban and rural schools;

Estela and Ernesto Bravo, whose continued assistance throughout the project was invaluable;

Lucile Lindberg, Mary Moffit, Peggy Schirmer, Sidney Schwartz, and Vivian Ubell, who read early drafts of the present manuscript and offered many valuable comments and suggestions;

Nancy Garrity and Ruth Lewis, who shared their own Cuban day-care experiences and insights with me;

Silvia Brandon, Silvia Carranzas, Jairo Chavez, Barbara Collins, Marcia Espinal, Henry Flacks, Marjorie Moore, Carol O'Flynn, Silvia Sánchez, Anita Whitney, and Ana Zapata, all of whom assisted me during various phases of the research for this book;

Judy Berkan, Olivia Stokes, and Roslyn B. Alfin-Slater, who analyzed specific aspects of Cuban day care;

Devorah Spencer, who suggested the title, and Cathy Alfano, who typed the manuscript not once but several times;

Kai Erikson, Carlos Díaz-Alejandro, Anthony Maingot, Nita Manitzas, Sidney Mintz, and Kalman Silvert, whose help was both concrete and vital, as they know;

Deans Jack Roberts and Marvin Taylor of the Department of Education of Queens College of the City University of New York, who not only consented to but helped arrange for the leaves of absence from teaching without which this project could not have been carried out;

James Cass of the *Saturday Review* and my publisher and editor, Richard Seaver, both of whom gave me early, and very vital, support.

Finally, I am deeply grateful to my friend and co-worker Robert Ubell. In addition to editing the manuscript, he has given without hesitation of his knowledge, experience, and concern. His probing questions, forthright criticism, and warm support did much to influence the content of this book. His suggested additions and changes have been incorporated in the text.

Sections of this work draw on conversations with many Cuban officials. Listed below are the names and positions of those who have been quoted directly, as well as those who have contributed background information on day-care education. They represent only a few of the many people in Cuba to whom I am indebted.

Dr. Daniel Alonso—head of research of the Children's Institute; also a member of the National Pediatrics Group of the Ministry of Public Health (MINSAP);

Dr. Max Figueroa Araujo—General Director, Center of Education and Development, Ministry of Education;

Dr. Arsenio Carmona—head of the Educational Psychology Department of the Ministry of Education;

Vilma Espín—President of the Federation of Cuban Women (Federación de Mujeres Cubanas) and President of the Leadership Council of the Children's Institute (Instituto de la Infancia);

Elena Gil Izquierdo—Director of Special Plans, Ministry of Education;

Dr. José A. Aguilera Maceiras—Vice Minister of General and Special Education, Ministry of Education;*

Dr. Consuelo Miranda—head of the Education Department of the Children's Institute, and Director of the Training Schools for Day-Care Workers (Escuelas de Educadoras);

* Died, Spring 1972

Dr. Abel Prieto Morales—General Director, Technical and Teaching Services, Ministry of Education;

Clementina Serra Robledo—National Director of Day Care Centers (Círculos Infantiles) and member of the Leadership Council of the Children's Institute;

Haydée Salas—Director, Plan Especial de Jardines Infantiles;

Lela Sánchez—Co-director, Plan Especial de Jardines Infantiles;

Marta Santander—National Sub-director, head of the Educational Department, Círculos Infantiles;

Lecsy Tejida—member of the Educational Psychology Department of the Ministry of Education; also liaison psychologist with the Círculos Infantiles.

This book was written with the help of a joint research grant from the Social Science Research Council and the American Council of Learned Societies, and a teaching and research grant from Yale University.

Portions of the present work have appeared, in somewhat different form, in the *Saturday Review*.

MARVIN LEINER taught for many years in the Bedford Stuyvesant and the Bushwick sections of Brooklyn. He has a Ph.D. in Elementary Education from New York University. At present he is Professor of Education at Queens College of the City University of New York, and he formerly was Lecturer in Latin American Studies at Yale and Fellow of Trumbull College, also at Yale. Dr. Leiner and his three children spent the 1968-1969 school year in Cuba, where the children, then aged sixteen, thirteen, and seven, all attended Cuban schools. The author's daughter Karen also worked in a Cuban day-care center during her year there and kept a diary of her experiences, parts of which are included in this volume.

Dr. Leiner is currently editing a book entitled *Children of the Cities: Education of the Powerless*, and working on a second volume of his study of Cuban education, which will deal with the system from first grade through the university years.

A RICHARD SEAVER BOOK
THE VIKING PRESS, 625 MADISON AVENUE, NEW YORK 10022

CHILDREN ARE THE REVOLUTION

The first act of the story of early-childhood education in Cuba follows a rather simple plot. In the beginning—before the Revolution—virtually no program existed. Former President Fulgencio Batista, who did very little for the Cuban population in general, did even less for the children.

With the coming of the Revolution, those sections of the population that had been most neglected in the Batista days suddenly found themselves in stage-center: the poor, the women, the blacks, the peasants, the workers, and the children. The Stanford University political scientist and Cuban expert Richard Fagen notes that the new government of Fidel Castro placed its major emphasis on the children of the Revolution "as the prime movers and beneficiaries of the new society." [1] The script of the Revolution called for righting the social wrongs of a sorry history; had a well-written scenario been all that was required to make Cuba prosper and progress, the play would have had a happy ending.

But life does not always mirror plays. For the Cuban people, once the Revolution had overturned the old regime, the full extent of the Batista legacy suddenly and frighteningly became apparent. Economic, social, and educational retardation persisted. Poverty, ignorance, disease, waste, and bureaucracy turned out to be the real threats to Cuba's future. The Revolution in itself, of course, was no mean accomplishment; but when the revolutionaries took control, they were immediately faced with an even more herculean task than waging war. The Revolution had really only begun.

A physician who writes a prescription assumes that there is a drug store in the neighborhood to prepare the medicine. But what if there is no pharmacy, no druggist, no medicine? Only a prescription signed by Dr. Castro and his revolutionary team? So it was with the Cuban people. In the case of Cuba's plans for early-childhood education, the problem was especially poignant. Consider what one needs to start a day-care system. Classrooms: Cuba had no facilities worth mentioning. Teachers: there were hardly any (and many of those who had taught school before the Revolution had fled with the coming of the Castro regime). Books, materials, administrators, psychologists, teacher-training institutes, curricula, menus, chefs: the inventory is staggering. All the past may be prologue, but for revolutionary Cuba the past was a vacuum.

Richard Fagen suggests that "the overriding theme of the Cuban Revolution is change. Its leaders seek a new society, one organized from the ground up on principles different from and often diametrically opposed to those of the preceding regime." [2] Had the revolutionary rhetoric failed to fire the Cubans with hope, and had it offered no tantalizing promise of the days ahead, the revolutionary dream would have turned into a debacle. Instead, the Cubans took Dr. Castro's prescription and attempted to fill it. Whether the Cuban educational medicine is an appropriate cure for its historical pathology, whether the Cubans can come up with a cure to arrest the diseases spread by the previous system is, in part, the theme of this book.

The story of Cuban early-childhood education is instructive on many levels. It offers those who are concerned with developing nations a glimpse at what can be done with the education of children in emerging countries if funds and resources are combined with dedication and commitment. The education of poor children in Cuba offers educators concerned with teaching in the cities and rural areas of the United States and elsewhere a microcosm wherein to study some of its methods and strategies, and judge its results. Finally, what the Cubans are doing with infants, pre-school children, and day care—the entire range of early-childhood educational activities—offers research workers, educators, psychologists, and communities everywhere experimental evidence of what is possible in the education of the very young. The Cuban experience with early-childhood education may go a long way toward answering some of the fundamental questions now being raised in this sensitive and controversial area.

Cuban day care has already achieved the kind of international prominence usually reserved for the great powers in education such as the United States, England, China, and the Soviet Union. Despite Cuba's economic handicaps and the need for investment in many other areas, the revolutionary government decided to initiate and offer massive support to a large and comprehensive day-care program. Far ahead of much of the world, Cuba's fledgling program offers many innovative features unknown in countries richer and far more educationally and economically developed.

Compare the number of children in day-care centers in New York, for example, with those in Cuba. The population of Cuba is roughly equal to that of the five boroughs of New York City. Latest available figures show that eighteen thousand children are enrolled in some form of day care in New York; Cuba has fifty thousand children in its early-child-care centers. Consider, too, that New York offers far more day care than do most other sections of the United States. Many countries have no programs at all or programs on so small a scale that little can yet be learned from them. Day care is still often thought of as some form of charity, or at best a system of communal babysitting or custodial effort.

The Cubans can be proud of these essential and far-reaching features of their day-care system:

Cost. Cuban day care is offered free to families with working mothers.

Accessibility. Largely on a first-come, first-served basis, child-care facilities are open to all who apply, depending on the availability of space.

Infant care. Centers admit babies as young as forty-five days old and continue care through age five.

Single administration. While in most countries day care, nursery school, and kindergarten are administered by different agencies, the Federation of Cuban Women holds the single responsibility for all preschool programs.

Health services. Not satisfied with offering only custodial services, Cuban day-care centers provide continuous medical treatment, preventive health care, and proper nutrition for all children.

Paraprofessional staff. Unable to staff day-care centers with professional personnel, the Cubans nevertheless opened facilities, relying on relatively inexperienced and untrained young people for staffing.

Community involvement. Parent education and participation is part of the day-care system. In addition, the centers draw on the support of other agencies and neighboring factories, offices, and farms.

Day care in Cuba is part of the island's commitment to expanded schooling on all levels, from the *círculos*—the day-care centers—to continuing education for adults in the factories. One of the primary goals of the Revolution in Cuba—which has suffered from a centuries-long lack of education—is to develop an educational system offering a variety of opportunities. The Cuban early-childhood education program, therefore, is only the first step on the road to educating the entire population.

I ★ GOALS

In almost every phase of contemporary Cuban life there is a set of principles upon which action is based. Pre-school education is no exception. Early-childhood educators have enunciated three tenets on which their programs are based: 1) the liberation of Cuban women from the exploitation and chauvinism of the past, 2) the development of the new Cuban man, and 3) the consequent social and economic benefits day care offers the community at large.

THE LIBERATION OF WOMEN

In Cuba before the Revolution, as in most parts of the world, women were an oppressed segment of society. When there was work, women were traditionally relegated to menial positions in the homes of the wealthy and in U.S. and other foreign-dominated business interests. When not participating in the economy outside the home, working-class women managed family life. Middle-class women, even those who were educated, often found little or no access to the mainstream of economic life beyond their own doorstep. According to the 1953 census, women accounted for only 17 percent of the total Cuban labor force. Those women who worked participated only in areas traditionally acceptable for female employment. Among professionals, 80 percent were elementary school teachers. Women in industry were concentrated in the textile, food, and tobacco sections. More than a quarter of the total number of working women were employed as domestics.[1]

The reason for the disproportionately low number of women in the work force was twofold: most women were not prepared to perform any but the most menial jobs, and there was no provision for child care to permit women to work outside the home. Inez Orfano, Director of the

O. Raúl Pérez Círculo Infantil, recalled her experiences in pre-revolutionary Cuba:

> Do you know that almost no woman could work before? Rather, the women who could work before were those who could study, who were middle-class. There weren't *superación* [in-service] courses for women on all levels of education as there are now. You had to have a politician friend and do political work for him and then perhaps you'd get a job, sometimes a *botella* [padded payroll job in government].
>
> There used to be families where the man earned very little money; they had a number of children, but the mother couldn't go to work because there were no nurseries where she could leave her children.[2]

The lack of adequate child care before the Revolution perpetuated this system: many mothers kept their older daughters home to care for their younger children, which contributed to the large school drop-out rate. Many girls between the ages of ten and twelve, who acted as surrogate mothers, were forced to disrupt their studies and leave school.

As in most of Latin America, in Cuba women reflected their position in life as seen through the eyes of Cuban men, who had been nurtured in the spirit of *machismo*—the Latin notion of male superiority and aggressiveness. This concept dictates that the woman be enigmatic and saintly, and that her life be lived through her strong, earthy, virile male. He, on the other hand, can fulfill his sexual fantasies apart from her, but he must fight—even to the death—in defense of her "purity." Susan Kaufman Purcell of the University of California at Los Angeles (U.C.L.A.) notes: "Premarital relations or infidelity in marriage, while unacceptable in women, not only was accepted, but was encouraged in order that the male attain the ideal of the *macho*—the virile, daring, forceful, and self-confident male." [3]

While the woman was expected to be a model of virtuous and modest behavior, she was clearly subservient to the man. Patriarchal and authoritarian, the ideal family structure demanded that the wife and mother be kept at home. To work was beneath her dignity; to compete in public life, a disgrace. The man was never subject to these constraints.

The highly stratified class structure in pre-revolutionary Cuba allowed only upper-class women to hope to approach the ideal of "femininity," while middle-class and peasant women were prevented from achieving this ideal. Of course, poor women had to do their own housework and were often forced to do menial labor for others in addition to their chores at home. Nevertheless, the double standard and the subordination of women to men permeated all classes. "While the lower class women could not conform to the feminine ideal," Purcell acknowledges, "poverty was perfectly compatible with *machismo.*" [4]

Among its many revolutionary goals, the Cuban Revolution sought to alter the role of the woman in society, to destroy the traditional condition in which women found themselves. Fidel Castro, calling for an alteration of the role of women in Cuban society, proclaimed: "Women's participation in the Revolution is a revolution within a revolution. And if we are asked what the most revolutionary thing is that the Revolution is doing, we would answer that it is precisely this: the revolution that is occurring among the women of our country." [5]

Cuba required that women join the revolutionary effort for pragmatic as well as egalitarian and moral reasons. The Cuban economy, stripped of its professional classes by the upheaval of the Revolution, nevertheless geared itself for dramatic expansion, which required large-scale increases in its labor force. It became immediately apparent that women would be needed to augment the existing labor supply if the new demands for more goods and services were to be met. The conventional approach which kept women in the home could not be accepted if the revolutionary economy was to expand. The goal of women's liberation, in Cuban terms, was the inclusion of women in the labor force. The Revolution facilitated this participation by creating mass women's organizations, adult education, and day care, which would allow women to leave the home to go into the factories and fields. "Society has a duty to help women," Castro pointed out early in the Revolution. "But at the same time society helps itself considerably by helping women, because it means more hands joining in the production of goods and services for all the people. As is well known, *one of the means to make it possible for women to work is the creation of day nurseries.*" [6]

In order to fill the need for child-care services, the Federation of Cuban Women (FMC), the nationwide mass women's organization which the new regime had established in 1960, initiated in 1961 wide-scale day care of the children of all working women in Cuba. Created through the union of a number of smaller women's groups, the FMC is led by Vilma Espín. Initially, the membership of the FMC totaled less than 100,000; by the autumn of 1971, more than 1,300,000 women belonged. Designed to encourage women to participate in the Revolution by educating them to their role in the new economy, the FMC offers a variety of consciousness-raising, politicization, and educational activities. Its most important activity, however, is the Círculos Infantiles, or day-care center program, which it administers. The purpose of the nursery school is "to take care of the children of working mothers, free them from responsibility while working, and offer them the guarantee that their children will be well cared for and provided with all that is necessary for improved development." [7]

Cuban day-care centers are flexible enough to render services for a broad spectrum of working mothers. The círculos accept children from the age of forty-five days until they are ready to enter the elementary schools directed by the Ministry of Education. Most are open six days a week, from 6 A.M. to 6 P.M. Others offer more extensive schedules permitting women to work late in the evening. Some allow parents to leave their children around the clock during weekdays; on weekends the children return home. Until quite recently, an alternative child-care system, the Jardines Infantiles, also offered universal free nursery facilities for preschoolers. Now being merged into the FMC-sponsored círculos, the Jardines Infantiles were set up mainly for children in the large cities. Despite the considerable hostility at the start from Cubans who feared that day care would "sovietize" their children, the current demand for early-childhood centers far outstrips available space.

The cost of organizing, equipping, staffing, and training for the círculos is considerably greater than that of day-care efforts in most other countries. In terms of its effect on the Cuban economy, however, it is a price worth paying. "We have learned," Castro has said, "that the entire nation profits from the incorporation of thousands, of hundreds of thousands, say of a million women into production; if each one of those million women produces the value of a thousand pesos per year, a million women means a thousand million pesos in created wealth. And what does it matter if society forgoes receiving the part that they pay for day nurseries?" [8]

Through day care and other efforts to engage women actively in the economic mainstream of the country, the total number of women employed in productive labor more than doubled in the six years from 1964 to 1970.[9] Following a recent visit to Cuba, U.S. author Elizabeth Sutherland reported: "The landscape of Revolutionary Cuba was not a man's world. No longer were women the janitors, caretakers, and consumers of the society, but its producers and organizers." [10] Women are now found in many positions, from agricultural workers to car mechanics, from dentists to department store clerks.

Nonetheless, many Cubans still view women as most suited to certain jobs. While women account for the largest share of preschool and elementary teachers, they comprise only a small percentage of the total enrollment in engineering schools. They may serve in the military but are not subject to the draft. In heavy industry, women are given selected tasks considered proper for female skills and position, while other jobs are open only to men. Much of the economic role offered to women in present-day Cuba is often supplementary and often substitutional. That is, they are often enlisted in the work force to replace men in such tasks as that of waiter and kitchen help in restaurants, to permit men to go on to more "productive" areas. In this connection, Purcell points out:

The Castro regime has made little or no effort to refute many traditional notions regarding the particular suitability of certain roles for females. Women still are expected to have primary or sole responsibility for domestic and child care in the home. . . . There appears to have been little effort made to change the prevailing stereotypes regarding certain kinds of occupations as being more suitable for females.[11]

Some women have found their way into posts of authority, yet none supervises essentially male activities. Women do occupy supervisory positions in areas where participation by women is great. Vilma Espín is in charge of the Federation of Cuban Women and Clementina Serra directs the Círculos Infantiles. Nina Fromenta, Minister of Light Industry, is responsible for a government agency which has under its jurisdiction the textile industry, 80 percent of whose work force is female, and the workers in the plastics industry, half of whom are women. Another female minister, Raquel Pérez, is head of social welfare, which also has a large female labor force.[12]

Sexual equality may be doctrinally appropriate for the Revolution, but it is not yet an integral part of the consciousness of Cuban men and women. The concept of machismo is still strong, even among younger people. Women can choose to work or not and can rely on the father or husband for support if it suits them. Even if she does work, the Cuban woman often feels the necessity of conforming to the traditional female role in the household by doing all the cleaning, cooking, and child-rearing chores.

The goal of the Cuban day-care program is to free women from these traditional constraints. In the words of Clementina Serra:

Círculos infantiles permit a great majority of mothers to free themselves partially from tedious housework which frequently impedes their permanent development and improvement. Women who are tied down by housework end up enclosing themselves in a world so limited that they lose contact with life itself—living at its margins and reducing their scope of interest to the solution of never-ending daily needs. In this way, they daily narrow their vital areas, hold back their development and exchange living for routine vegetating.

When the woman can project herself into her environment, widen her circle of interests, incorporate herself into creative work, and establish multiple relationships which enrich her intelligence, we are giving her the opportunity for complete development, to fill each minute of her existence with worthwhile content. In other words, we are giving her the opportunity to realize herself totally as a human being.

When a woman fully integrates herself into her social environment she learns, among other things, the whys and wherefores of the functioning of her society, and consequently how she should guide the conduct of her children in this respect. Also it widens her knowledge of the education of children and the best way to achieve it. Both things, the awareness of the goals and the knowledge of the means, permit the woman fo fulfill her obligations with greater efficiency, although possibly reducing the number of hours of direct attention given her children. With less time, there will be greater educational achievements because the conduct of the mother in the home and in society (making itself felt more positively by the quality rather than the amount of time) is decisive in the education of a child.[13]

THE NEW CUBAN MAN

The primary goal of the Revolution, as articulated by Fidel Castro, is the creation of the new Cuban man—a fundamentally humanistic, altruistic, concept of the human being, which combines classical Marxism, collective consciousness, and the view that people are perfectible beings.[14]

In a July 26, 1960, speech, Castro outlined the key points in Cuban Communist ideology and what it means with respect to the formation of *conciencia*—or what one sociologist defines as "an amalgam of consciousness, conscience, conscientiousness, and commitment": [15]

In a Communist society, man will have succeeded in achieving just as much understanding, closeness, and brotherhood as he has on occasion achieved within the narrow circle of his own family. To live in a Communist society is to live without selfishness, to live among the people and with the people, as if every one of our fellow citizens were really our dearest brother.[16]

Much has been written about the new socialist man in Cuba and elsewhere in the socialist world.[17] Theodore Hsi-en

Chen, writing about the new socialist man in China in the *Comparative Education Review*, reports:

According to the Communists, the old society breeds individualistic and selfish persons motivated by feudalistic and bourgeois loyalties. They think of personal benefit and personal ambitions. Their narrow family loyalties encourage selfishness and the neglect of what is good for the general public or the state. The new man will be collectivist, utterly selfless and ever mindful of his obligations to the revolution and the Communist party. Until the old man is replaced by the new, the proletarian way of life cannot prevail and the new society must remain a dream.[18]

For Chen, the characteristics of this new human being will consist of absolute selflessness, ideological study, love of labor, versatility, and expertise in socialist construction. With only minor variations on that theme, the new socialist man in Cuba will exhibit similar traits.

The conceptual framework of Cuba's *hombre nuevo* is the humanistic ideal, and its source is Marxist ideology. In "The Economic and Philosophical Manuscripts of 1844," Marx offers the view that man is essentially a free creative spirit with powers that enable him to produce for the sheer pleasure of doing so.[19] In agreeing with Marx, Castro believes that once work is no longer an exploitative function, as it is under capitalism, it will become an artistic creation. Castro asserts that the meaning of the Cuban Revolution is in releasing man's spiritual energy in a society where he will be able to cultivate the life of the mind and exercise his creative abilities freely in his work. At the end of a day's work, the Cuban citizen will devote his leisure to the pursuit of cultural and scientific activities.[20] In the speeches and writings of Ernesto (Che) Guevara and Fidel Castro, the new man is motivated by a sense of solidarity and brotherhood among men; he finds fulfillment in his work and respects work as being worthwhile in and of itself; he shares the fruits of his labor with all of his countrymen; and he exhibits strong personal and moral character coupled with individual responsibility and intellectual curiosity.[21]

Círculo officials Consuelo Miranda and Marta Santander echo the views of Castro and Che.[22] According to these leaders, the new Cuban man will be: a healthy individual, with a new attitude toward work which will allow him to identify it with the pleasure of creation and social duty rather than with a salary; a man without selfish feelings, a generous man with a sense of the collective and of his duties with respect to it; a man capable of joining in solidarity with all men who suffer exploitation, regardless of where they were born; a man who will arrive at these convictions through his own reasoning and who can adjust to discipline for identical reasons; and a man capable of defending his beliefs at all costs and ready to fulfill every task with responsibility.[23]

Cuban schools, sparked by this revolutionary vision, are given the responsibility of painting appropriate images of the new society in the child's mind. Believing that the school environment is instrumental in altering attitudes and developing new perspectives, Cubans trust the school setting to change pre-revolutionary attitudes toward collectivism, socialism, work, and man's role in society. By encouraging collective living, group rewards, and "anti-egoist" psychology, the schools play a dynamic role in the alteration of society. Much is made of "collective consciousness" in Cuba; the Marxist-Leninist philosophical basis of the Cuban system leads inevitably to an appreciation of the collective principle throughout Cuban society, including early-childhood education.

In the círculos, the group—rather than the individual —often takes the central position. For example, there are collective birthday parties at which all the children born in a given month celebrate their birthdays together.[24] Such parties are the custom not only for day-care and kindergarten children, but for young adults studying to become teachers in the Makarenko Institute.

Miranda noted during one of our interviews: "We feel that no exceptional child should be singled out. That means that if there is a child with outstanding qualities he should be part of the group too. For example, we had a school which Che's children attended. Naturally, when foreigners came, they were interested in seeing them, and often the *asistentes* [teaching assistants] would show off by bringing out Che's little boy." When Miranda discovered what was going on, she instructed the school to discontinue the practice immediately. "We do not wish to single out any one child, because it will deform his personality. We try to cultivate modesty. There are some children who are very intelligent or lively or likable—which is all very good—but they should not be singled out." Miranda indicated, however, that Cuban schools do not seek completely to submerge children into the group. "We must develop personal initiative. We must develop to the utmost the capabilities of the oustanding child, but we do not want to make him feel superior to the other children despite the fact that he may indeed be." [25]

Collectivism in the schools is not designed exclusively for the children. The collective spirit is also cultivated in teacher training, and even textbooks, manuals, and lesson plans are products of a joint effort. Often, no single author is given credit for a project.

To train children for their future role as new socialist men and women, collective consciousness begins the moment the child enters the círculo. When a Cuban baby is placed in a playpen, he is not put into a standard U.S.-type model with room enough only for himself or at most one other baby. The Cuban playpen—or, more appropriately, "corral"—permits at least six infants to play together in a space equal to the size of a small room. Based on the Soviet or Eastern European model, the corral, raised on coffee-table-high legs, offers children the chance to interact with their asistentes practically face-to-face. Far more practical than the U.S. playpen, it does not force adults to bend to floor level to reach the children.[26]

Group play takes precedence over individual activities. Nancy Garrity, a member of a team of Boston educators who visited Cuba during the summer of 1970, reported: "In older children's rooms in day care centers most activities seemed to center around a child working as a member of a group or for the good of others. Much of the child's time is spent in circle games and activities. Often, one child or the teacher is in the center and the other children work as a group." [27] Encouraged to design activities to stimulate group play, asistentes lead children into social and play patterns to help them develop collective attitudes. Generally, children are not even permitted to play by themselves; asistentes make special efforts to see that all children participate in the program designed for the collective. This concentration on the group rather than the individual in the early years is an essential part of the effort to form the collective consciousness of the future *hombre nuevo*.

The spirit of collective action is not new to Cuba. Basically an agricultural society, Cuba has always been characterized by the extended rather than the nuclear family. Such large, rural families embrace not only the parents and their offspring, but grandparents and often aunts, uncles, cousins, and other relatives. Forced to develop a common purpose because of their economic position, these extended families form a collective bond.

For revolutionary Cuba, Miranda suggests how, in

theory, Cuban educators believe they can develop a new
consciousness among nursery-school children. By weaving
into the curriculum and the everyday classroom life such
concepts and behavioral patterns as sharing, respect for
work, responsibility, modesty, and self-discipline, Cuban
educators feel they can assist in the creation of the new
Cuban man. Miranda gave her views on these key elements:

Sharing. In accordance with the social regime which Cuba has established, we must form collective conscience. How do we do it?
We do it with a life shared in common which permits the continual
formation and execution of habits of sharing, cooperation, and living together for the achievement of a common objective and the
common enjoyment of successes and happinesses.

Children celebrate their birthdays together; they do everything
together. If there is a party, it is for everyone. Birthdays are cele-
brated in common for all who have their birthdays in the same
month. Thus, there is a unity in the happiness of the community.
The parties are at the same time. They go on trips together, they
have conflicts with people together, they have good times together
with good friends, and in bad company they have bad times
together. This is the only way for the child to achieve identifica-
tion with his group and override his individual-egotistic interests
for the collective interest. But he must have a strict formation over
a long period of time in order to feel part of his group. We are sure
that this is the way it works; we see it work, and for this reason this
is how we develop our círculos.

We can see easily that the children can give. Even in the age
groups where they usually want to keep things for themselves, if
they see another child crying, they . . . give things to him. Of
course, this is imitative of what the teaching assistant does. If they
see that an asistente gives a crying child a toy in order to calm him,
they tend to do the same thing. You will see how they frequently
take what they have and give it to the unhappy child to console
him. Soon the time comes when he is "lost" in the group. Of

course, his individuality is not lost—that is something else—what is developed is the collective conscience.

Respect for work. We use every situation and chance which in one way or other leads to the creation of a conscience favorable to work and respect for work. For this reason, we hold graduation in the countryside. He who is well-behaved, who has studied well, who has received good grades—he will have the honor of going to work in the fields. It's like a prize. Rather, he begins to identify work not as a necessity nor as a salaried job, but as something pleasurable. Then we take the children to the fields and they, for example, pull weeds. We spend all day there. He who works very hard will be put in the "service brigade" to serve his friends at the table. This is his prize. Of course, we also use this method with the un-disciplined: "If you behave nicely you can . . ." Then we have the child accept and know the workers. We have a party there in the country and the children honor the workers, give them flowers, and recite poetry.

Responsibility. We try to stimulate personal incentive, persever-ance, work responsibility. We give the girls tasks. For example, we invite the older girls to help with the little ones; but we take care that we invite them and that only those who wish come. "Now, remember if you come you must finish everything." We give her the feeling that she must do what she promised to do well, but as a game. "Let's go and play asistente. If you don't want to, don't go. If you go, you will be the asistente. If you go, you must do your job." This is the principle we have. And they begin to acquire responsi-bility. We tell them it is good if they want to help their little friends but that there are certain things they must do, that the game has certain tasks that must be done. We are trying to create responsibility.

Self-discipline. We also wish to develop the acceptance of a cons-cious self-discipline to embellish his conduct. For example, we have a series of habits in the círculo regarding order. We want the child to learn to follow these habits because he is conscious that they are good for him. To convince him, we say the following things: "If you put away your own clothes, the *compañera* [comrade] who is taking care of you will be able to take you out to play more quickly." It is good for the group that each member of it do his part because it is for the good of all. If we want to slide and we fight to see who gets to go up first, we must stop because we cannot let the children fight to climb up; they might get hurt. The best way is for them to stand one behind the other so they can enjoy their time more. The time spent fighting is lost. Then the child begins accepting because he is conscious that this is good for the community, for his group. These are the fundamentals of what we consider a conscious discipline. Things are accepted because the group definitely benefits from them. The acceptance of a conscious discipline is considered basic for the kind of man we hope to form.

The things I have mentioned are all thought of as basic for this new man. Of course, there are other things we develop in the círculos, but these are the main things because we hope that they will produce a healthy man with a new attitude towards work— identifying it as pleasurable and a social duty instead of for salary; a man stripped of selfishness; a generous man with a feeling for the collective and his duties toward it; a man capable of feeling solidarity for all men who suffer from the exploitation of the powerful, no matter where they come from. He will be a man who arrives at these conditions by the use of his reason, because we are trying to develop his powers of reasoning so that he understands reasons and he adapts to a discipline for identical reasons. A man capable of tenaciously defending his convictions, capable of responsibly fulfilling his duties. This is what we hope to form and we do all we do as the initiation of this formative process which would then be continued.[28]

In creating the foundation for the new Cuban man, Cuban day care naturally incorporates the political content of early-childhood education. Children are reminded of roles played by their national heroes, particularly those who died in the revolutionary struggle. For example, the *planea-*

miento—curriculum guide—of the círculo education department suggests that in the sixth week of the fall session, children are involved in a thematic program called "Our Friends the Guerrilla Fighters." The staff is encouraged to perform certain activities, not only to develop in the children a sense of patriotism and communal spirit, but to provide opportunities for learning experiences in language arts, memory, thought, attitudes, and habits. These are some of the suggestions for classroom activities for four-year-olds during this week:

Show pictures of guerrilla fighters. Explain in a simple way how these companions fought in the mountains to liberate their nation. Tell them that Fidel, Camilo, and Che were also guerrilla fighters. Have the children learn the verses of the Cuban National Anthem. Tell of the events in the life of a guerrilla fighter. Talk about Che and how he wanted children to be. Have the children learn the *Hymn to Che*. Carefully observe the pictures of the guerrillas. Comment on what the guerrilla fighters are doing. . . . Have the children recall various facts about Che's life that have been talked about during the week. Have them recall and identify hymns taught during the week. . . . Awaken admiration and respect for our heroes and leaders. . . . [29]

On one visit to Havana, for example, on Camilo Cienfuegos's birthday, children from all the círculos were taken to the Malecón and Alejandro rivers to throw flowers into the water as part of a ceremony commemorating this revolutionary leader who was lost over the sea on a flight to Havana. The *Hymn to Che* and other revolutionary songs and poems are taught in every círculo in Cuba. In addition to their homage to Che and Camilo, the schools focus on a few selected national heroes going back to the nineteenth century such as José Martí and Antonio Maceo. Nursery schools discuss and dramatize the battles of the Mambises and the *Granma* landing. Stories, poems, and suggested art projects published in the monthly educational magazine *Simientes*, as well as in educational plans, guide the schools on how to inculcate concepts related to Cuban socialism. Typical of such curriculum aids is a story published in *Simientes* entitled "The Selfish Campesino":

Once upon a time, near a big city, there lived a *campesino* who was poor, very poor. He and his family had to work very hard just to have enough to eat, and it wasn't unusual for them to go to bed hungry.

When the Revolution triumphed, Juan, as the campesino was called, began to work on the farm nearby. In time, he was able to buy a cow and some hens, forgetting at times how poor he had been before.

Some time passed, and in the area where Juan lived they began to build a school for lots of children. Besides learning, the children would see television, and eat, and even take their baths there.

The man in charge of construction came to see Juan to explain that he would have to move to a new house which would be given to him because the spot where his shack stood was to be part of a great sports field that was being planned. But Juan didn't even want to hear about it and said he wouldn't move because he had a cow and he couldn't take her to the new house.

Juan's family was very sad because they had seen the new houses which were really pretty and had light and water and even new furniture. But Juan refused to move.

One day a little old man who also lived there came to see him. Because the old man had lived so many years, he was very wise.

After greeting Juan he asked him:

"Do you like to eat bread?"

"Yes," Juan answered.

"And when your shoes wear out, do you like to buy new ones?"

"Yes," he answered again.

"And when you're sick, do you like the doctor to take care of you?"

"Yes," he answered, puzzled by so many questions.

"Well then, just think. If the baker didn't make bread, you wouldn't have any to eat; if the shoemaker didn't make shoes, you would have to go barefoot; and if the doctor didn't study a great deal, he wouldn't be able to cure you when you're sick and you would die. And this is the way we receive something every day from the work of others which helps us to live better. But you nonetheless don't want to help make all the children who will go to this new school happy, just because you don't want to leave an old cow that you didn't have before and that you really don't need."

Juan didn't say anything, but he kept thinking and thinking, and very early the next day he gathered his things together and moved. He felt very happy now, even though he no longer had his cow, because he knew that he too had helped make it possible for many children to learn to read.[30]

Life in other socialist countries is also part of círculo political education. Information sheets, stories, and pictures are sent to the círculos to help asistentes teach the children about other countries, in order to develop what the Cubans call "international consciousness." Miranda insisted that even young children can develop an international consciousness. "First we must teach the child to believe in Cuba and his homeland, so that he can understand that other children can love their countries and that there are other countries in the world. If they have no concept of their own country, they can have no concept of others." Miranda noted that at the círculo level, visitors from other nations help in this educational process. "When a Vietnamese visits we tell the children that he comes from a very distant country, that he is a friend who suffers greatly, that his family has suffered greatly, that he must struggle. When an Indian from South America visits, we tell the children something of his life; we may demonstrate the theme in puppetry; the children may see a movie." Naturally, Cuban

schools emphasize the parallel between Cuba, other socialist countries, and the underdeveloped nations of the world.
The lessons make much of children who "suffer most as a
result of imperialism." [31]

In one of the "pedagogical orientations" designed to
promote socialist character, we discover how the Cubans
feel they can initiate the first steps, at the nursery-school
level, in the creation of the new Cuban man:

1. When we prepare simple programs in memory of our country's heroes—the country's founders and builders of today and yes-
terday.

2. When we speak of the beauty of our country and we show the
children photographs or use other means which permit us to help
them to understand and love the beauty of the countryside, of the
sky, of the sea, of the trees, of the rivers, etc. This will be done at
an opportune time and separate from the routine.

3. When we teach them songs and poems fit for their age
groups, in which we foment love of the homeland and admiration
for its natural beauty.

4. When we take advantage of any opportunity to let them know
of the famous men Cuba has produced in the fields of science, art,
literature, sports, etc.

5. When we tell them of the men who made the Cuban Revolution possible and emphasize their talent, valor, and honesty.

6. When we tell them of the life of and sacrifice of life for the
betterment of his country of the martyr after whom their círculo is
named.

7. When we have programs to salute children of other national-
ities and countries which are struggling like Cuba for a better
world, and when we hail the heroism of the people of these countries.

8. When we teach the children folk songs and dances from other
countries, and when we begin to develop in them an appreciation
for the beauty of these things.

9. When we dramatize the customs of other countries.

10. When we cut out pictures from magazines of various countries and have the children observe and appreciate the beauty in them.

11. When we invite children from other countries who live in Cuba to spend a day at the círculo and become friends with the children there. The children themselves organize and prepare the welcome.

12. When we take advantage of conditions such as those presented by Children's Day to refer to the universal fraternity which should guide relations among men and which is begun by fraternity among children.

13. When we teach the children that there are groups of men who impede this fraternity and explain why they do this and whom they represent. It is easy to present this to children through the use of puppets.

14. When we take advantage of every opportunity to inform them of news events.

15. When we ask them to express through drawings the beauty of their country, its defense, its sources of production, or any other direct or indirect ideas that develop love of one's country and national pride, universal love, and fraternity, and repulsion and disdain for imperialism and its representatives.[32]

BENEFITS TO THE COMMUNITY

In addition to its economic, social, and revolutionary benefits, day care provides a series of practical benefits which are having a profound effect on Cuban society:

Bringing the revolution to the countryside. As in most Latin American countries, in pre-revolutionary Cuba the difference between the standard of living in the urban centers and the rural sections was shocking. Since the Revolution had its genesis in the countryside, the Cuban leadership dedicated itself to returning the benefits of the Revolution to the countryside. With the construction of day-care facilities in the remotest parts of the country, and with the introduction of early-childhood education to rural, back-woods areas, the círculos are playing a major role in eliminating the differences in standard of living between town and country.

Nutrition and health care. Among the many services that Batista neglected to provide for his people was an effective system of health care. Day care in Cuba, together with other programs, has attempted to rectify this omission. The círculos have become one of the best vehicles for delivering medical and nutritional care to children.

Compensatory education. Faced with a largely "disadvantaged" population, the círculos immediately offered a program of "directed" learning which attempted to compensate the child at school for what he might have failed to receive at home. Day care became the first crucial step in eliminating the difficult transition from poverty and deprivation to the new technological society.

Community and family education. As part of their program to provide a wholesome atmosphere for the child, day-care leaders insist on bringing the family and community into the educational process as well. Cuban child-care centers encourage families to participate in school affairs and in addition offer intensive courses and guides on child rearing.

Day-care centers form a hub for family needs by providing children with proper nutritional and health care and offering parents guidance. Outside organizations also become active in early-childhood education through a system of voluntary aid teams. Factories, offices, and farms "adopt" círculos and provide services the school itself would otherwise find difficult to obtain. In short, the círculos attempt to educate the family and the community on the importance of the child in Cuban society and the círculos are aided in turn by parent and community involvement.

In the long run, the Cuban experiment will not be judged on whether Cuban educators articulated their goals properly or whether they were searching enough in their analysis of their own society to provide judicious goals to be followed by their young. Rather, it will succeed, in the eyes of the world, and in the Cubans' own estimation, if their children become productive, responsible, creative, dynamic adults, if the new society is peopled with a kind of human spirit capable of surviving the social, political, and economic challenges of the future. If their children are locked into the psychological and moral precepts of the past, incapable of offering creative solutions to problems dimly emerging beyond the pressure of present demands, it will have failed.

According to Fagen, Cuba's approach to the re-education of the spirit of its people "has been directed toward an attempt to create new values and behaviors in the context of the new political setting. . . . In Cuba there has been a planned attack on the cultural fabric itself." Fagen emphasizes that "the test of the new Cuban man is how he behaves—whether or not he works, fights, studies, cooperates, sacrifices, and contributes in the prescribed manner. . . . The regime seeks to forge the new political culture in the crucible of action." [33]

Charles Silberman, whose *Crisis in the Classroom* stirred national reaction to educational failures in the United States, reminds us of the need for principles, yet cautions that principles must be followed if they are to have meaning:

Talking about morality, honesty, or kindness in no way insures that people will act morally, honestly, or kindly. The job of the educator is to teach in such a way as to convert "ideas about morality" into "moral ideas." In the words of the Talmudic axiom, "Let not thy learning exceed thy deeds. Mere knowledge is not the goal, but action." What educators must realize, moreover, is that how they teach and how they act may be more important than what they teach. The way we do things, that is to say, shapes values more directly and more effectively than the way we talk about them.[34]

Yet the lack of clearly articulated goals in the United States is seen by some as an obstacle which must be hurdled. As David Rosenham has observed, "We who are the planners, preachers, and implementors in American education have nothing to say about the premises that underlay our work." He raises the question whether or not the present turmoil in American education has so shaken our values that it is next to impossible to arrive at a meaningful set of goals. Or, as he asks, is it perhaps "that no value consensus can be arrived at in a democracy such as our own that stresses individualism and the right of each man to have his own values?" Or worst of all, is it that "we have no values, that we traveled the American educational scene by the pragmatic seat of our pants, that we are carpenters rather than creators, implementors and not ideators?" The ultimate question, of course, is: What shall our values be? [35] Urie Bronfenbrenner believes that goal-oriented activities require broad acceptance of the aim to be achieved, and consensus on the behavior necessary to achieve those goals. Cooperation, therefore, is not only critical but essential. In the absence of goals, hostility reigns, disorientation presides, and alienation is achieved.[36]

It may turn out that the goals of preschool education can be fulfilled successfully, if they remain modest. As Katherine Read has suggested, day care should first of all encourage the child to like himself, to develop self-respect, and to feel loved and valued. Second, the child ought to develop a sense of being an independent person capable of asserting himself. And finally, the child ought to be able to follow the urge to explore, discover, and create, to master the world of things around him.[37]

For the Cubans, the test of the efficacy of their early-childhood education program is whether or not they have succeeded in instituting the goals they have set for themselves. While the number of schools available does not yet meet the demand, the Cubans feel that this is only a passing stage. Cuba is rapidly heading in the direction of satisfying its quantitative needs. The growth of early-childhood education facilities over the past decade strikingly testifies to Cuba's sincerity, enthusiasm, and financial commitment. If the Revolution survives its other major challenges, it will provide the largest day-care program per capita in the world.

Whether Cuba's early-childhood program, together with its other educational, social, and political aims, will succeed in sculpturing a new Cuban man out of the clay of the past is a difficult question to answer, at least at this stage. But, as the following chapters will document, it does seem that the sculpture is taking shape. In the words of Samuel Bowles, "Cuba has become a huge school, and the Revolution itself is the teacher." [38] Much of the spirit of Cuba's goals in educating its young is expressed in a banner seen at an educational conference in 1969: "We work for children because children know how to love, because children are the hope of the world."

II★PERSONNEL:
THE PARAPROFESSIONAL SOLUTION

After my first visit to Cuba, I reported that "The exodus of the country's middle class on those flights from Havana to Miami had nearly depleted whatever meager literate resources Batista had ungraciously left behind. Never before had a socialist revolution permitted its fat cats to flee in such numbers and with such license." [1] Cuba's educated class fled from the Revolution as from a burning building. Richard Jolly reports that in the first three years following 1959, probably 250,000 Cubans, including large numbers of professional workers, left the country. About one-third of Cuba's physicians emigrated, and perhaps 15 percent or more of its technical and professional personnel. [2]

This exodus coincided with the new revolutionary government's plans for drastically expanding education. Thus the lack of trained personnel immediately became critical. The universities suffered as much as early-childhood education. "At the same time that our need for teachers and professors increased with the expanded educational opportunities offered by the Revolution, the number of qualified teachers decreased sharply," commented Consuelo Miranda. [3] Of those who had been educated and had not left Cuba, many were hostile to the regime and refused to participate in its new educational programs.

Lacking a pool of educated young people to join the new early-childhood educational system, the Cubans turned elsewhere, tapping the resources of their largely uneducated teenage population and of older women whose previous experience had been in their own homes raising their own children. Consequently, the pioneer asistentes in Cuban day-care centers had meager training and a very low scholastic level. At Castro's suggestion the círculos at first employed *manejadoras*—nursemaids—who had served middle-class children. As anyone who lived in pre-revolutionary Havana can testify, the parks of wealthy sections of

Vedado, Miramar, Country Club, and Biltmore were filled with these white-uniformed, uneducated girls from the farms. Choosing to work as nursemaids rather than as prostitutes or servants, these country girls cared for middle-class children. All that these nursemaids brought with them were their home child-rearing practices.

The staffing of day-care centers with a largely paraprofessional staff was unprecedented in the annals of education. While ostensibly a sixth-grade education was required, the círculos at first permitted women to work without even meeting that minimal standard. This was particularly true for centers in the countryside, where the general level of education was even lower than in the cities. Only recently have the standards been raised to the point where an eighth-grade education is required for asistentes. Day-care paraprofessionals are not called teachers, nor are they considered to be teachers. The centers do employ kindergarten teachers who work under the direction of the Ministry of Education; they perform traditional classroom duties for children of kindergarten age. A typical círculo employs one teacher to approximately twenty asistentes.

Provided with free uniforms and shoes, asistentes routinely work six days a week and on Sunday often do "voluntary work" at the círculo or elsewhere. Those who are on the 6 A.M.-to-2 P.M. shift have breakfast, a snack, and lunch at the school. Workers on the 11 A.M.-to-7 P.M. schedule receive lunch and an afternoon snack. In 1969, círculo asistentes earned $82.47 per month, regardless of how long they had been employed.

At first, asistentes were offered minimal remedial-training courses. Even these were often cut short in order to fill posts at círculos, which were opening at a faster rate than training schools could staff them. After the círculos were well established, asistentes were required to achieve greater scholastic proficiency. Some outstanding asistentes were taken from the círculos and sent to school for a year to study such subjects as liberal arts, child care, child psychology, and nutrition. Upon returning to their círculos, they were expected to guide the other staff members.

The first school of directors for círculos infantiles was founded in January, 1961. The 300 who enrolled were the first boarding students (*becados*) of the Revolution. A month later, 1300 pupils enrolled in the school of asistentes—the first training center for women who care for children in the círculos. Selected from former domestics and peasants, boarding students were required to have at least a fourth-grade education.

On a visit to one Havana training school for asistentes, the Escuela: Formación y Superación de Círculos Infantiles—School for Development and Training in Day-Care Centers—I observed that work in the day-care centers was balanced with studies at the school. Students studied for three months at a time in groups of twenty-six students; classes were held Tuesdays through Saturdays, with Mondays set aside for "productive or agricultural work." Rather than select model círculos in which to teach students, those with normal working conditions were chosen. The classes consisted of practical training in Spanish, mathematics, rudimentary child development, health care, and arts and crafts.

Of the 109 women who had entered the program, only 46 remained after a year. While some had dropped out of their own accord, many students had been persuaded to leave after consultations with the cooperating círculo personnel and training staff. Some had left simply because they did not like children; others had been asked to leave because they were not considered to be well suited for working with children; and still others had quit because they discovered that the work was too hard. Not displeased with the high drop-out rate, the school believed that its program permitted those who were not cut out for the work to leave before they were assigned to a círculo on a full-time basis.

At this school I attended a Spanish class taught by Dr. Edilia Blanco Sánchez, whose major responsibility was as a consultant on technical and professional training at the Ministry of Education. As a shortage of adequate personnel exists on all levels of the Cuban educational system, she was pressed into service in the classroom. An exciting and dynamic teacher, she displayed a dramatic style. Using a letter Che had written to Fidel,[4] she wove into the lesson grammar, revolutionary idealism, Cuban history, and the needs of the círculo.

Most training of asistentes, both in the early days and now, is provided by continuous in-service courses. Given to all asistentes who have not attained acceptable levels of formal education, these classes offer fairly rudimentary concepts of child development and growth. In-service training prepares asistentes in what the círculos call cultural, technical, and political categories. Organized under the Worker-Peasant Education courses, the cultural program provides women with their minimum sixth-grade educational requirement. Technical sessions are held under the leadership of the director of the school and offer training in materials, teaching, psychology, and other day-care matters. For the political section, study circles cover current events and discuss materials presented by the Communist Party, the Union of Young Communists, and the Federation of Cuban Women. These groups meet about every fifteen days, during the children's nap period. At first, these improvement courses had been offered at night, but the hardship of getting to class at the close of a long day was too great. It is worth noting that in-service training is given not only to those who deal directly with the children, but also to cooks, cleaning women, and others who work in the círculo.

In 1970, the círculo leadership concluded that better training and higher qualifications were necessary if standards were to be raised. To this end, they opened three new four-year day-care training schools, Escuelas de Educadoras.* The one in Oriente trains círculo personnel for that province as well as for part of Camagüey. Another, based in Havana, serves students from the provinces of Havana, Pinar del Río, the Isle of Pines (Youth), and Matanzas. The third, in Las Villas, covers that province together with the other part of Camagüey. By autumn 1973, the Oriente and Havana schools had begun their fourth year, and the school in Las Villas was in its second year.

Entrance requirements call for an eighth-grade education. Students between the ages of fourteen and twenty-five are accepted.[5] Applicants must also be members of the Federation of Cuban Women "since we cannot have anyone lacking Revolutionary conviction involved in the formation of the new generation." [6] The círculos recruited student teachers by visiting secondary schools throughout Cuba to inform them of the new program. Eighth graders were invited to visit círculos and, as a result, some 225 were registered. The limited number of students enrolled in the Escuelas de Educadoras reflects the círculo's intention of keeping these schools functioning as small pilot projects until they can be properly evaluated and adequately staffed.

The curriculum not only offers day-care workers-in-training courses related to future professional activities, but also provides a general education, including liberal arts and sciences. Professional courses include general, early-

* For a description of new developments in the Escuelas de Educadoras, see Chapter VI, Cuba Revisited.

childhood, and developmental psychology, as well as educational and vocational psychology. Pedagogical studies cover reading and arithmetic (which have been initiated on an experimental basis in some círculos). In addition to taking courses in art, dancing, and music, students are taken to concerts, ballets, recitals, and art exhibits. Study of a musical instrument is mandatory.

Asistente training proper begins in the second year, when the students observe at day-care centers. In their third year, they perform some supervised activities and, in the fourth, undergo daily, intensive training and practice. In this last year, asistentes-in-training spend fifteen days each month in the day-care center and fifteen days at school. They practice teach at the same círculo throughout the final year. Under the direct supervision of the head of the círculo, each student, before graduation, will have had at least sixteen to eighteen weeks in a day-care center, with full responsibility for a group of children. The regular asistente is present at all times during the student's sessions at the center.

Current plans call for a coordinator to be assigned to the círculo to facilitate the integration of new asistentes into the center. The directress will continue to supervise students on a day-to-day basis.

Contemporary psychologists understand that one of the basic requirements of children is to establish affective relationships with adults who care for them. This is vital for the child, whether the adult happens to be his mother or the woman who cares for him at a day-care center. We know that if the child does not feel loved and properly cared for, he will not develop the kind of trust required for his socialization into the group; if he receives consistent and understanding attention from the day-care worker, he will be better equipped to deal with others. Trust in others brings confidence. Therefore, a chief criterion in selecting day-care workers is that they be warm, affectionate, and capable of dealing with children in loving, maternal ways.

Turning an uneducated teaching staff into an effective group of paraprofessionals is not easy for the círculo leadership. Ideally, women who work with children should have an appreciation of childhood development and psychology so that their interaction with them will be based on a clear understanding of what can be expected at different age levels. Unfortunately, in practice, despite their best intentions, asistentes are often ignorant of the basic developmental needs of children. Marta Santander relates an incident which occurred in a Camagüey school:

When I tried to explain that a toddler of two and a half should be taught to dress and undress himself and fold his clothes and put them away, one of the women said to me, "Poor little things. How can I make these little children do it? It's so hard for them. It is much easier for me to do it for them." Then I had to explain that teaching the children to do it for themselves would be much more work for her, and that it was the only way they would learn and develop. Some still insisted that they felt sorry for the little ones, and that they preferred to dress and undress all the children, even though it was a lot of work for them. I had to spend a good deal of time explaining to them what this meant in terms of retarding the children's development at that point, and preventing them from moving on with the next steps in the program.[7]

Because it is not possible to hire asistentes who have achieved acceptable levels of scholastic ability, the jardines and the círculos depend on their assessment of personality and accept only those who will at least not cause emotional damage. "If they had an education as well it would be ideal; but since they do not at least we try to select those who are healthy." [8]

Both jardines * and círculos expect their workers to be warm and generous. If jardín psychologists discovered that those who were seeking employment were rigid or authoritarian, they were not accepted. Prospective teachers were given psychometric tests to determine their personality and to weed out those who, the jardines felt, would be harmful to the children. "But even after all the tests, what counted most was our interview," Lela Sánchez, co-director of the jardines, explained. "We were interested in the picture which emerged when we met them face-to-face. During the interview we could determine whether the person was intelligent and whether her personality was suitable." [9]

The jardines, in their search for the "healthy" day-care worker, attempted to screen out those who exhibited obsessive characteristics. "We reject the obsessive person because she is always concerned with whether the child will fall and what if the child gets dirty; she inhibits children." [10] Those diagnosed as depressives and "impulsives" were also rejected—depressives because they limit the child's ability to express joy and impulsives because they agitate children by screaming at them. Applicants considered "pacific" were embraced. Recalling one woman who at first glance might have been rejected by more formal acceptance procedures, a jardín psychologist said:

At one school we have an older woman, the first one to work in the plan. About fifty, she is like a grandmother; she is calm, peaceful, relaxed, and affectionate with the children. She may have a sixth-grade education, but what she brings, in terms of how she relates to the children, is quite positive.[11]

Nancy Garrity observed that asistentes "seemed like women who were relying on their common sense to deal

* For a full description of the alternate day-care program, the Jardines Infantiles, see pp. 104–117.

with groups of children and didn't have any storehouse of ideas or activities or theories to fall back on." [12]

The círculos also understand that educated professionals may not be essential ingredients for the best preschool educational system. As Miranda points out, women who work with children need not have advanced educational backgrounds to deal effectively with children. Unschooled paraprofessionals usually do not view children with the detachment of some educators who feel that their responsibility to children is a duty and not a pleasure. "A woman without so much professionalism, but who offers great affection is of much more help," Miranda said. "I'm not interested in whether or not the people who work with the children are university graduates. If you employ someone who has a degree, she may turn out to lack affection and human warmth. Who wants them, even with their higher education?" [13]

In a search for a scientifically sound method for screening those who work with children, two young Cuban educational psychologists delineated the elements that affect the child's development and established criteria for filling those needs. In the Cuban professional journal *Psicología y Educación*,[14] Sergio León and Franklin Martínez, outlined four elements that determine the character and personality of children: biology, culture, environmental stimuli, and interpersonal relationships. Among these influences, the last—"the personal history of the experiences of the individual with others"—is the most significant, "since personality is, in its major part, a product of social learning in the interaction of the child with the family, other members of his group and social attitudes." León and Martínez indicated that the formation of personality through these interpersonal relationships takes place during the child's first five years of life.

Because the people employed at the círculos and other

early-childhood programs exert a major influence on the development of the children's personalities, León and Martínez undertook to find out the kind of people who should be permitted to work with young children. They developed a series of tests to discover the right kind of person and to exclude the wrong.

First, they established four criteria required by all children: 1) solid, positive, consistent, affective relationships between the child and his parents or the person in charge of him; 2) stimulation of independence, curiosity, and freedom to play and explore with adequate affective support; 3) socialization and education through learning based on good affective relationships, respect, and guidance of the child's initiative; and 4) a good pattern or model of conduct which allows the child to acquire positive characteristics and reactions by imitative behavior or indirect learning.

Based on these criteria, the Cuban researchers defined the kind of person who could best be expected to deliver these essentials of good personality development. People who work with children should be able to establish "solid, pure loving relationships." They should be able to stimulate and reward "independence, autonomy and curiosity" by tolerating the child's exploration, experimentation, and free play with loving approval. Adults should be able to put themselves in the child's place, that is, understand that the "child is not an adult" and know the child's "limitations and possibilities." Finally, "aggression and rejection should be absent as much as possible" from the personalities of those who are to work with the young.

The questionnaires and tests developed by these psychologists were originally designed for kindergarten teachers. To my knowledge, they have not been administered by the círculos, the jardines, or the Ministry of Education. Nevertheless, they are of interest because they reflect the kind of concern Cubans feel about this area. It is note-worthy that these psychologists, in their absolute focus on the needs of the children in the classroom, purposely ignore some of the character traits that the revolutionary ethic requires of all its citizens. As León and Martínez remind us, their object is to focus on only one aspect of the potential teacher's personality, her ability to work with children.

We are not considering other factors of the individual's personality except those related positively or negatively to such work. This means, for instance, that in answer to the question "What are the three things you like to do best?" if the subject answers, "Do productive work," that answer—although from a political and social point of view is very positive—has a neutral value [inasmuch as we] are not interested in registering militancy but ability to work with children.[15]

The answers to León and Martínez's questionnaire listed below—positive, negative, and neutral—were selected at random from those given by people seeking jobs as teachers.

The following expressions would be considered positive and would indicate that the prospective candidate would work well with children:

"I chose this work because I like children."

"I like children; I feel happy with them."

"I would like to be a teacher."

"I love my children and I have the highest feelings for them."

The following expressions, on the other hand, are considered negative and would indicate that the candidate would not be suited for such work.

"Most children are silly."

"I chose this work because I needed any kind of work."

"Kindergarten is easy to work in."

"Marriage, the home, and children are absurd."

The next examples are considered neutral and would not be used as a basis on which to judge the character of a prospective teacher:

"I would like to study sculpture and painting."

"I like classical music and the movies."

"I like foolish conversations."

"Children are born to be happy."

In selecting classroom personnel, educational systems elsewhere in the world rely in large measure on objective scholastic achievement tests, the number and variety of education courses one has taken, and an hour count tallying up to an arbitrary total of days, weeks, and perhaps months of time spent as a student teacher. Only rarely do educational systems assess a teacher's personality. Is her character suited for working with children? Is she kind? Does she understand the needs of children? Does she feel affection for children? Will they put their trust in her? These basic questions must be raised. It is not enough for someone to have taken all the proper courses, passed all the tests, and put in all the hours. Without a fundamental sense of caring and a healthy disposition toward children, the teachers who are chosen might at best be as ineffective as another leg on the desk, and at worst, as damaging as a policeman's nightstick.

It is to Cuba's credit that, in principle, the day-care leadership appreciates the critical importance of this issue. Whatever educational route the Cuban day-care centers finally take—directed learning, laissez-faire, or some other mode—the quality of the teacher will tell.[16] No educational system has much chance of success if those who work therein are funneled into the classroom as numbers on a license.

Once selected, the asistente is offered elementary literature on the role she should play. Asistente training in the
in-service coursès, and even in the more advanced four-
year schools, concentrates on establishing an understanding among the women concerning the need for warm, affective relationships between them and the children. Realiz-
ing that the educational level of the asistentes is often not
advanced enough to grasp sophisticated psychological
theories, the in-service círculo classes are content to give
modest lectures in simple language. These cover basic
steps in child development—sensory-motor, language, and
social behavior. Examples are drawn from asistentes' experiences within the círculo.

Dr. Consuelo Miranda is director of the asistentes' educational section in the training school. She commented, "We
explain that these characteristics [basic steps in child
growth] develop simultaneously, but we separate them so
that the asistente can understand each process better. We
caution them that anything they do can affect not one, but
all these aspects. We explain these things in a non-scientific
vocabulary." [17] Psychology is taught as one way of establishing an affective relationship between asistentes and
the children.

Stressing affective relationships, Miranda recommends
that asistentes show their faces to babies in the crib as much
as possible, and say a few words to each child as often as
they can, even though the words themselves may be of little
consequence. She also suggests that asistentes try to make
the children laugh whenever they can, and that they should
become familiar with and be able to distinguish the child's
different types of crying, and how he shows anger and fear.
In general, they ought to know and interpret what the child
needs and when he needs it. Miranda says that this can be
achieved by caring for the child with love. "There is no pos-

sible excuse for letting a child cry a long time without going
to his side and trying to calm him." [18]

Miranda suggested ways in which this may be explained
to the unschooled asistente:

Now how can you do this? When the child cries, you don't let him
cry. Mothers don't do this. When he cries they go to see what is
wrong. This is what you want to do. If he is cold, you must cover
him; if he is hot, you must move the crib to a cooler spot; if you
think he is tired of the position he is in, you must move him; if he
is hungry, give him food; if he is thirsty, offer him water; if you
think he is frightened, carry him, hug him a little, cuddle him,
hold him close to you and say sweet things or sing, and then put
him back in the crib. This relationship must be established, very
directly, because what we are teaching them is very clear, things
that belong to the various periods of psychological development,
but taught, as you can see, without nuance, stripped of scientific
vocabulary—as if it were a conversation. If we were to explain this
in other terms, they would not understand it.[19]

Asistentes are instructed to be resourceful in developing
play activities for older children when they are not involved in group play. Asistentes who offer children toys
must first teach them their use and then participate in the
game for a few minutes. After the age of three, group interaction becomes important for the child's own attempt at
socialization. Miranda notes that "Separation from the
group constitutes a punishment for the child whose conduct
is not adapted to the group in one way or another." Miranda
cautions asistentes to be careful in their use of this sort of
punishment: "It is not advisable to abuse this punishment,
but in certain circumstances the asistente can separate the
child from the group when he disturbs the rest.[20] She con-
cludes with an admonition to all asistentes, reminding them
of the critical importance of warm, open relationships between children and adults:

Inasmuch as coldness and lack of affection produce disturbances characteristic of anaclitic depression which leads to serious consequences in the child's future life, every assistant should offer love and tenderness to the children in her care. For her children she will be the "adult" who directs and gives security to their first social contacts, the "adult" who will not fail the little one, but who will attend him lovingly in every moment.[21]

David Rosenham, remarking on the similar Soviet emphasis on warm teacher-child relationships, reminds American educators to be aware, "as we revise our own curricula for young children, that care precedes technique, that positive regard is a necessary ingredient for intellectual maturation." [22]

In staffing both the círculos and the jardines entirely with women, Cuba reflects the traditional view that women are the only proper caretakers of very young children. Some educators do not agree with this view. Sánchez lamented the lack of men in day care:

It is a great deficiency. We ought to have men in day care. But if you consider the worldwide custom of relegating child care to the mother, the lack of men in the center is not that hard to understand. The feeling that women should have control over infant rearing is first of all purely biological in that she provides the infant's food. Once past this stage, the mother is seen as the source of kindness, warmth, and protection, this feeling having grown for centuries. Nevertheless, it is important for the child to be influenced by a man. The presence of a man in the household, especially in Cuba, is very important.[23]

The preponderance of females in the child's environments at school and at home denies boys and girls access to male models. The absence of men in school and at home during most of the day is not a problem in Cuba alone. And, as in other countries, it does not appear likely that the current leadership will alter the situation. When asked whether men can be hired as círculo asistentes, Marta Santander replied emphatically, "We don't need to place men in the círculos!" Her reasons? Children in day care receive enough attention from men in the street, in their home, and especially those who come to the center to perform such chores as gardening, plumbing, and maintenance. And, perhaps more importantly, "There are many fronts of work in this country, and men are very much needed. There are many jobs that women can do, but many others that they can't. The man working with children would have to be a young man. But young men are working on other important things." She assumes that "Men are not going to work with children when women can do it. And in any case, since children need affection and special care, it's hard to find this in a young man." [24]

The Cuban experience shows that if large-scale day care is to be implemented rapidly, school systems can at least call upon the untapped resources of community people to initiate the early phases of the program and, perhaps, to continue to be effective as the program matures. Experience with paraprofessionals in other countries offers only fragmentary indications of their success in the classroom. Studies in the United States with very small groups lead researchers to believe that paraprofessionals can serve many useful functions.[25]

For Cuba there was no real choice. If they were to embark on their ambitious program of day care, they could not wait while they trained certain people in their population to care for the children in the day-care centers in a manner that would meet minimal standards in more advanced countries. They had to plunge ahead, making do with what they had to work with in actuality, while developing educational theory and a more sophisticated staff apace.[26]

III ⋆ THE SCHOOLS

CÍRCULOS INFANTILES

Before the Revolution, no early-childhood education program of any consequence existed in Cuba. The only facilities were thirty-seven crèches operated for children between the ages of one to six. These programs provided mainly for the children's physical care—food, shelter, and the like. With virtually no educational goals, the crèches admitted children whose families could either muster political influence or provide favors to government officials. Most Cubans considered children in the crèches as charity cases, "needy" children. Day care in Cuba before the Revolution largely mirrored the approach followed until recently in the United States. As U.S. day-care expert Bettye M. Caldwell points out, day care historically took the philosophical position of offering "care and protection for children from families with some type of social pathology." [1]

Although a kindergarten program existed before the Revolution, it served only a small section of the urban Cuban population. In rural areas there were no kindergartens at all. No public school programs for children below kindergarten age existed, except for so-called charity orphanages, like crèches. Castro has contrasted the Batista educational legacy with the achievements of the Revolution:

All of us have undoubtedly seen many schools appear in the countryside. Before the Revolution there were not many; there were only a few schools in rural areas. Certainly a great part of school-age children in the country were without schools or without teachers. With the advent of the Revolution, first came the teachers and, wherever possible, a school was built. Eventually, teachers were sent out to all the children in the countryside. Anyone would have considered this a great triumph; anyone would have considered this a great advance because there has always been a great clamor in the countryside asking for schools, asking for teachers. Whenever a teacher arrived there was rejoicing. A new school was always greeted with joy. And for any country on this continent to receive a teacher, a school, has always been a reason for rejoicing.[2]

Origins and Evolution

Post-revolutionary early-childhood education began with close ties to the goal of women's liberation; the círculos infantiles were organized under the direction of the Federation of Cuban Women. During the first five years of the nursery school system under Castro (1961–1966), FMC members in each locality were responsible for making clothing or securing educational materials. In July, 1966, the Ministry of Industry assumed these responsibilities.

Originally the círculos operated five days a week, 6 A.M. to 7 P.M. Changes over the years in the scheduled day-care hours reflected the growth and alterations in the Cuban economy itself. As more women entered industry, late afternoon and evening hours were offered. Especially after the 1966 "push" into agriculture, two important changes were introduced: the Monday-to-Friday schedule was broadened to include Saturday as well, and a limited number of círculos offered twenty-four-hour sleep-in care.

Today círculos operate year-round, providing free day care for all children—on a space-available basis—from forty-five days to six years of age. Five- and six-year olds in the círculos are taught in the kindergarten under the Ministry of Education. From 1961 to 1967 the centers charged a nominal fee. Círculos provide free clothing (uniforms) and all meals—breakfast, lunch, snack, and dinner—during school hours. Cuban mothers receive maternity leave from their jobs six weeks prior to and six weeks following the birth of their children.

Speaking in 1967 about what day-care centers will offer, Fidel Castro said, ". . . the infant may attend a children's nursery from the age of one month, beginning when the mother's maternity leave is up and she returns to her job. The children's lives will be perfectly organized; they will receive the best of care." He continued: "They will enter the nursery early in the morning and return home late in the afternoon." [3]

In 1966, after the first phase, three new and different types of schools were established. The first covers the great majority of the centers in Cuba today. Called *externos*, these facilities function only during the day, usually from 6 A.M. to 7 P.M. with students going home after dinner. Garrity reports that in one of these externos in Varadero, many of the parents were drawn from the tourist industry, which calls for long and irregular hours. "Parents can schedule their use of the day-care services according to work schedule needs," [4] Garrity observed.

The second type, the *interno*, or boarding school, operates from Monday to Saturday, with the children sleeping in. Children in these centers usually visit with their parents one day during the weekend and spend their holidays with their families. This boarding care is designed for the children of parents who work away from home or who live in inadequate housing. Sleep-in care, however, is not encouraged. Very limited in number, internos represent only a fraction of the total day-care picture.

The third kind of day-care facility, the *mixto*, or combination school, houses both the *externo* and *interno*, with most of the children going home at night, while the others sleep in. Of the 364 círculos in Cuba in 1969, 272 were externos, 29 internos, and 63 mixtos.

Table 1 shows the relative distribution of círculos in the six Cuban provinces and the Isle of Youth, and indicates the number of children enrolled in each during 1968–1969. Table 2 presents the growth of the círculos throughout Cuba from 1961 to November 1970. By September 1971, the total number had reached 436,[5] serving more than fifty thousand children. The most recent data available indicate that in the fall of 1973 there were 610 day-care centers.[6]

Organization

The círculos are closely tied to the Federation of Cuban Women on all levels—national, provincial, and regional— and the Secretary of the Círculos Infantiles in the FMC is

Table 1: Círculo Enrollment by Province (1968–1969)		
Province	Centers	Enrollment
Camagüey	40	4,040
Havana	146	22,370
Isle of Youth	6	476
Las Villas	50	4,734
Matanzas	28	2,938
Oriente	70	7,576
Pinar del Río	24	2,112
Total	364	44,246

SOURCE: Clementina Serra, "Report on the Círculos Infantiles," mimeographed (July 13, 1969), p. 6. At the time of this report, there were also 30 círculos in construction and 67 projected in national Círculos office plans.

also the Círculos' National Director. She is Clementina
Serra, one of the few women on the Central Committee of
Cuba's Communist Party. Although noted for her organiza-
tional skills and revolutionary commitment, she readily
admits that she is not a professional educator and that she
constantly turns to educational leaders and psychologists
for guidance and direction.

The central administration of the círculos is organized
into four major parts, each with its own director. The sections are: 1) organization, which includes *emulación*—
socialist competition—and evaluation; 2) education, which
includes pedagogy, psychology, and training of personnel;
3) economics, in which are subsumed planning, supplies,
investments, and statistics; and 4) the Department of Diet

Table 2: Círculos Infantiles (1961–1970)

Year	Centers	Year	Centers
1961	37	1966	194
1962	109	1967	262
1963	144	1968	332
1964	157	1969	381
1965	166	1970 *	430

* Through November
SOURCE: Marta Santander and Consuelo Miranda, "Círculos Infantiles: la educación en la edad temprana," in "Seminario interdisciplinario de educación permanente," mimeographed (Havana,
1970), p. 10.

and Health, which supervises hygiene, food, and medicine, and whose administrator works closely with the Ministry of Public Health (MINSAP). There are círculo offices in each province, whose divisions correspond to the national model. In some provinces medical and health supervision is coordinated by the provincial pediatric health unit of the Ministry of Public Health; in others, a group of technical advisers services each círculo by visits, supervision, and evaluation.

The círculos themselves are divided into these four basic age groups:

lactantes (bottle-fed babies)	45 days–18 months old
parvulitos (toddlers)	18 months–2½ years old
párvulos (nursery school)	2½ years–5 years old
pre-escolares (kindergarten)	5 years–6 years old

The lactante group is further divided into sub-units of three months. It should be noted that not all círculos offer lactante care.

Staffed by about thirty people caring for some 150 children, a typical círculo personnel list looks like this:

1 kindergarten teacher *
1 director
1 sub-director
19 asistentes
4 kitchen workers
2 cleaning workers
2 laundry workers
1 nurse
1 physician (who visits two or three times a week)

* The kindergarten teacher, a Ministry of Health employee, teaches the kindergarten-age children only.

Physical Plant

Cuba's warm climate, which had helped to build her tourist trade before the Revolution, turned out to be an enormous asset for the revolutionary regime as well. This is particularly true where school construction is concerned. In temperate or northern climates, schools must be equipped for cold as well as for mild weather. Proper heating systems and protective insulation is unknown and unnecessary in Cuban school-construction programs.

The warm weather also plays a role in the curriculum. In contrast to schools in northern climates, many activities may be enjoyed outdoors. Cuban children often play for long periods on patios and grassy areas outside the schoolhouse itself.

Many schools are housed in former homes and other pre-revolutionary facilities that have been converted into classrooms. The conversion program began after the original plan to offer new buildings for nurseries failed to meet the exceptionally large demand for círculo facilities; the program began in 1962. Built to national guidelines, newly constructed schools which were being built simultaneously with the conversion program offer play areas, fresh air, and large kitchen facilities. However, when the former homes of the pre-revolutionary middle and upper classes are used for schools, the facilities vary in their degree of effectiveness and adequacy. I visited círculos housed in former "railroad" flats where the children at the front had to go through each room in order to reach the small outdoor garden in the rear.

Often, where temporary facilities do not provide enough space, nearby parks and other outdoor areas are used. On the other hand, many large Havana mansions housing círculos provide spacious yards, gardens, patios, play areas, kitchens, classrooms, and bathrooms. In one such house, a garage was converted into the laundry room, and an upstairs suite was transformed into a rest area with cots.

Conversion of housing into appropriate facilities for schools and other community activities is a very efficient technique which provides prompt access to needed space and can meet standards set by specialists of highly developed nations. Frequently in the United States—particularly in central cities—the creation of nursery schools and daycare centers is hampered by the view that only new buildings will satisfy both educational principles and the needs of teachers and children. Creative use of vacant structures, as is done in Cuba, offers a means by which architects can convert town houses, markets, apartment buildings, offices, and other space into effective educational areas.

The first newly constructed centers opened on July 26, 1961—three in Camagüey and two in Havana. Built to accommodate 150 children each, these spacious nurseries were expensive to construct. Called Type A, they were often overenrolled and had as many as 200 children.

The second kind of facility, Type B (with a prototype built in San Andrés, Pinar del Río, at the westernmost end of the island), including large outdoor play areas, was smaller than the earlier centers. The key difference between the San Andrés facilities and the others was that the new style offered a centralized kitchen and laundry capable of servicing five separate círculos.

Type C, another model, built in Gran Tierra in Oriente province as well as in several other districts, is smaller than the other styles and has independent services for food, clothing, and laundry. Each accommodates approximately 120 children.

The most recent style, Type D, is the small *rústico*, located in small villages in the countryside. It houses 30 to 40 children, largely serving the needs of working farmers.

The círculo leadership considers the ideal size for newly built facilities, where population warrants it, to be 100 to 200 children.[7]

Fidel Castro, speaking at the dedication of the first five schools in San Andrés de Caiguanabo (Pinar del Río), reported:

Each school has been located according to the distribution of population, always with an eye to the most wholesome conditions and the most suitable sites, near the homes of the children who are to attend the schools and nurseries. Our architects and planners visited each site; working with them was a team of comrades who have been put in charge of the overall plan.

The installations are of magnificent quality. We must congratulate the architects who worked on these installations. Sunny and airy, healthier installations than these cannot be imagined. . . . The nurseries . . . have a section for infants and a section for older children, indoor and outdoor facilities, where they can move about freely.[8]

Others who have visited Cuban círculos recently came away with much the same favorable impressions as I. One report notes, "All the centers I saw were light and airy. Patio space was used extensively. If the center itself did not have grassy areas, children were taken to parks or to the beach." [9]

The círculo leadership reports that if classroom capacity were to double, there would still not be enough room to fill all requests. Under the pressure of community demands for more space, what is available is rationed according to a priority schedule. First preference goes to children whose mothers are employed in the agricultural sector of the Cuban economy. Children of teachers, nurses, physicians, and industrial experts come next. Third place is given to children whose mothers work in the service economy, while office workers are last on the list. Children of mothers who do not work get whatever is left. Miranda points out, however, that the priority is not fixed. "Of course, if a woman from any of the other groups has an emergency problem, we would take care of her child. If you are a secretary, for example, and you find yourself in a situation of real need, your child will be accepted in a círculo." [10] During the summer holidays, parents often take their children out of the círculo to accompany them on vacation.

Observations

Observers of any situation ought to reflect whatever is around them without distortion. Charged with the responsibility of recording the sights, sounds, and atmosphere of place, people, and events, they should act in the best traditions of objective journalism. However, the observer carries with him, in addition to his pen and pencil, tape recorder and camera, his own set of standards, beliefs, and experiences which alter his observations much as a pebble tossed into a pool of water alters its surface. During a year spent in Cuba in 1968 and 1969, and again on a visit in 1971, I spent long hours in the Cuban círculos in the cities and in the countryside, scribbling notes, taping interviews, and snapping pictures. To claim that my observations are wholly free from the inevitable distortion of subjectivity would be false, and would give the reader the impression that the events described here need no further comment. John K. Fairbank has observed, "The reporter is part of his report, like the historian of his history." [11] Thus, the reader must realize that while this report is as objective as I could make it, it is not impersonal.

In Cuba, as in all school systems, one finds vast differences between classrooms. As everywhere else, the adults in charge set the tone. While one day-care center director concentrates her attention on cleanliness and strict adherence to posted schedules, another is interested less in hygiene and more in play, less in routine and more in a relaxed atmosphere. One must always be wary of drawing conclusions about the whole system on the basis of observations made of one or even a few classes.

In general, the círculo day is a difficult one for the staff. Asistentes, women with a minimum sixth-grade education, must perform a wide variety of difficult chores—bathing, dressing, feeding, and cleaning. Often these duties do not permit the asistente to devote her time to free activities, which are designed to allow children to play and roam at ease. Painting, dancing, and singing take second place and programs offering cognitive development are frequently omitted entirely because of the pressure of routine. The círculo leadership is currently taking steps to introduce a variety of more intensive programs which offer the children activities tending to the development of cognitive skills.

Lactantes (Bottle-Fed Babies)

On one visit, I arrived in the morning to find the nine-to-fourteen-month-old lactantes outdoors. Their 8-to-9 A.M. activities took place in a safe, level grassy area outside the center— a quiet spot, removed from the rest of the school's activities. The children played with balls and other equipment. Two asistentes, who cared for eleven children, were busy supervising the play. One was with two children at a miniature seesaw, not more than four feet long; she was able to hold both children with her arms outstretched as they seesawed up and down. The youngsters loved it. While two others waited their turn, nearby a five-step slide was being used by other youngsters. Frequently, asistentes would sing or talk to the children, who were relaxed and having fun.

Although the schedule indicated outdoor activity from 8 to 9 A.M., I noted here no strict adherence to time charts. At 9:25 the children went into their classroom. They sat four to a table, either drinking by themselves or being helped with their water cups. Then each child was diapered in the small changing room, which was furnished with two tables and sinks with closets for diapers, towels, and other necessities.

While the older children rested on their cots, one asistente took care of a newly admitted twelve-month-old, who was not yet used to his crib. She stayed with him, singing and gently shaking his crib. The older children waited patiently while the younger ones were put into their cribs.

The large lactante room (approximately thirty-by-forty feet) contained about thirty cribs. Thirty box-like storage units stood against a wall. In the center of the room, a large, rectangular playpen (about five-by-ten feet) made of sturdy hardwood, with long, upright side poles, horizontal slats, and two large holes at both ends, stood at floor level. By far the most intriguing piece of furniture in the room was a giant crib, called a "corral," about six-by-fifteen feet, which served as a communal playpen. There was also a table with high chairs at each end. Nearby stood a small table with four chairs. Plastic toys and stuffed dolls sat atop the cubbies. The cribs, playpens, bunk beds, and other wooden structures are reportedly made by patients in the Havana mental hospital.[12] The lactante kitchen facilities, sterilization equipment, and rooms are completely set apart from the rest of the círculo.

At 10:05 A.M., while the nine-to-fourteen-month-old children slept, the six-to-nine-month-olds, who had been asleep for some time, awoke. The asistentes, after changing them, donned surgical masks to feed them.

At 10:40 A.M., the day-care physician entered the room to see if there was any need for his skills. On this particular day there were no problems, and he left shortly thereafter.

By then two of the nine-to-fourteen-month-old children had awakened. While the others slept on, the asistentes placed these two in the corral together.

Lunch that day for the nine-to-fourteen-month-old children included spaghetti, meat, cheese, compote, and milk. One child, who could not eat the "harder food," was given malanga purée with butter, milk, and meat purée instead. At lunch, two children sat in high chairs, and four older children sat at the table. An asistente moved her chair from one child to the next, helping each with his food, while two asistentes served. After a while, they traded positions. Soon after, one asistente tended to the tables, a second changed diapers and clothes in the dressing room, a third fed the smaller children, and another brought in more food.

As lunch ended, the youngsters began moving around the room: three played in the corral with plastic toys, one sat in a rocker, and another on the floor, and one stood near a table. Two sat on potties, and within five minutes six of the children had used the potties.

During the rest of the day, activities continued flexibly with asistentes providing warmth and attention. At this círculo, asistentes were especially sensitive to individual children. Generally, the child who cried was not ignored. Asistentes regularly picked up children and fondled them as they were changed, during mealtime, and at play. One asistente always seemed ready to attend to a particular child while the others were busy with groups. Efficiency and skill characterized their movements. Tables 3–6 show the schedule of daily lactante activities by age group.[13]

Although the day-care movement has accelerated nearly everywhere in the world, facilities for nursing babies are not common outside of Cuba. Only a few programs elsewhere offer such wide-scale care for babies as young as forty-five days. The círculo lactante program, as noted, provides complete services for children forty-five days to fourteen months old, including bottle feeding, diapering, napping, bathing, and all the routines traditionally practiced in the home. From my observations, and from the reports of others who have visited círculos in Cuba, the number of

---

Table 3: Daily Lactante Schedule (45 Days–3 Months)

	Time	Activity
A.M.	6:00	milk at home
	7:00–7:30	juice
	7:30–9:00	nap
	9:00	milk
	9:00–10:30	activity (sun)
	10:30–noon	nap
P.M.	noon	milk
	12:00–1:30	activity (bath)
	1:30–3:00	nap
	3:00	milk
	3:00–4:30	activity
	4:30–6:00	nap
	6:00	milk
	9:00	at home

Water: may be given any time.

babies receiving lactante care is low in comparison to the number of older children who attend Cuban day-care centers. Despite the availability of lactante facilities, Cuban families appear to be reluctant to entrust their infants to the care of strangers. In a society where most children are showered with attention and family affection, it is not surprising to find that parents are cautious about permitting the state to substitute for them. But babies who are enrolled in the lactante groups are handled with great care and affection. The women who work with them are instructed in

Table 4: Daily Lactante Schedule (3–6 Months)

	Time	Activity
A.M.	6:00	milk at home
	6:00–7:30	activity
	7:30–9:30	nap
	9:30	meal
	9:30–11:00	activity (bath, sun)
	11:00	juice
	11:00–1:00 P.M.	nap
P.M.	1:00	milk
	1:00–2:30	activity
	2:30–4:30	nap
	4:30	meal
	4:30–6:00	activity
	Water: three times daily.	

feeding, hygiene, language, and motor development, as well as the daily routine of caring for an infant. To avoid giving one child a formula prepared for another, an infant may never be placed in a crib other than his own. This procedure is followed so that when a substitute fills in for a worker who regularly attends the children, the substitute can easily manage the routines prescribed for each child.

Asistentes caring for babies in the lactante rooms are constantly reminded of the child's need for love and attention. "The loving atmosphere is most important." Urged to sing

Table 5: Daily Lactante Schedule (6–9 Months)

	Time	Activity
A.M.	6:00	milk
	6:00–8:00	activity
	8:00	juice
	8:00–10:00	nap
	10:00–noon	activity
P.M.	noon–2:00	nap
	2:00	milk
	2:00–3:30	activity (bath)
	3:30–5:00	nap
	5:00	meal
	8:30	milk at home
	Water: three times daily.	

songs and lullabys and to talk to the children, asistentes are encouraged to make every effort to insure that the children in their charge feel happy and wanted. "Don't let your children cry," they are cautioned. "It is a mistake to think that children cry because they are spoiled. Children cry for a reason and it is your responsibility to find out what that reason is." The asistentes are further admonished, "If you hear a child who cries continuously, you can be certain that the work going on in your salón is not being done properly, and we cannot consider it a good salón."

Asistentes are also urged to socialize with the children, to

Table 6: Daily Lactante Schedule (9–14 Months)		
	Time	Activity
A.M.	7:30–8:00	breakfast
	8:00–9:00	activity (sun)
	9:00–11:00	nap
	11:00–11:30	meal
	11:30–1:30 P.M.	activity (bath)
P.M.	1:30	juice
	2:00–4:00	nap
	4:30	meal
	4:30–6:00	activities
	8:00	milk at home
	Water: three times daily.	

encourage them to respond, and to create a personal rapport with them so that they "feel secure with you as the one who will satisfy their needs and solve their problems." To foster warm, affective relationships between the staff and the infants, the círculo leadership recommends that the women who care for the children bend over the cribs to let the children become familiar with their faces, sing or speak with the children as often as possible, play games with them, and set aside a few minutes every morning and afternoon to play individually with each child "without fail."

Encouraged to develop the child's language abilities, asistentes are told: "Never miss an opportunity when you are near a child to speak a few words." To help the children develop muscular control, dexterity, and coordination, the staff is provided with a manual of approved games and exercises, and they are instructed to practice with the infants daily. "And above all, let the infants move freely, clutch things, pull toys, throw things, climb ramps, etc."

While warmth toward children is a common phenomenon among asistentes, it is much more difficult for them to encourage independence in their charges. To this end, lactante workers are directed to allow children to eat by themselves so that by the time they move from the lactante section to the next group they will be able to eat at the table by themselves, drink from a cup, and sleep on cots. "It will take at least eight weeks to establish these habits." [14] Table 7 indicates the expected behavior patterns during mealtime for each age level.*

The círculos frown on infant habits such as the use of pacifiers and thumb sucking. Citing hygienic reasons for disapproving the use of pacifiers, Marta Santander said, "We

---

* For a more extensive discussion of mealtimes and nutrition, see Chapter IV.

can't always keep one child from taking it out of his mouth and another child putting it in his." During the first days of a child's stay in a círculo, he is permitted to use his pacifier if he has had one at home. Gradually, "with the cooperation of the parents," they take the pacifier away. "We are able to eliminate them—more or less—in a week!" Santander reported proudly. Similarly, the círculo frowns upon little pillows and pieces of cloth brought from home. These too are gradually taken away from the children. "We take them

---

Table 7: Expected Behavior at Meals

Age	Expected Behavior
9 months	Child learns to hold his own bottle. Child also holds his own cookies or toast.
12 months	A cup is substituted for the bottle.
14 months	Child introduced to chopped foods.
12–18 months	Child learns to use spoon.
18–24 months	Child learns to feed himself.

SOURCE: Interview with Marta Santander, Havana, 1971.

away slowly. When the child is asleep we take it away. The next day, we try to take it away sooner and the day after that we don't give it to him at all. In this way his adaptation won't be so painful." [15] Círculos only permit children to bring their own toys from home during the first few days of school. Afterward, the círculos prohibit toys brought from home.

Miranda agreed with her colleague as to pacifiers and thumb sucking. "Thumb sucking and pacifiers are prohibited in our círculos by the pediatricians for medical reasons and psychiatrists consider it a sign of emotional disturbance." Adding parenthetically that she herself did not consider thumb sucking an indication of emotional stress, Miranda confided that her own daughter had been a thumb sucker who had grown up to be "a perfectly normal person"! [16] Tough as the círculo leadership sounds in theory, in practice, many children do as they please. Even Santander laments that her own two-and-a-half-year-old nephew can't give up the habit: "From the first day on the child sucked his fingers. These habits are very difficult to stop." [17] Yet Garrity reports that she never saw any children who had graduated from lactante rooms with bottles or pacifiers.[18]

Despite the fact that group socialization is one of the principal goals of early-childhood education in Cuba, some observers have come away with the impression that the children in the nursing-baby units do not respond to interactive situations. As one visitor reported, after observing at the Varadero school, "Four children were put in a playpen together with six or seven rubber squeeze toys. There was occasional interest in the toys or in each other, but most interest was shown to passing caretakers [asistentes]." On another occasion, a visitor observed a situation in which six children were placed one by one into a large corral. As each new child was brought into the playpen, the others would concentrate their attention on the adult; some would try to touch her, others would squeal. When left alone, without the asistente present, the children would play with toys in the corral, largely ignoring the others in the playpen.[19] Lacking any systematic data on such behavior, Garrity nonetheless concluded that the goal of developing "cama- raderie" among children, through the use of communal playpens, did not seem to be successful. It appeared that the focus of the babies' attention was more often than not on a passing adult rather than on the other children. Garrity reports, "In no visible way did children turn to each other for support." [20]

While Garrity's findings suggest that babies have the ca- pacity for complex socialization in their playpens, it is more likely that infants in the lactante group acted as many chil- dren of that age do—they play "in parallel" and not with each other. Moreover, it seems fairly reasonable that babies should turn to adults in this kind of environment.

Plans and instructions can come to nothing if those who are entrusted to follow them either do not comprehend them or ignore them. "As Castro proclaims the dawn of the New Cuban Man to enthusiastic crowds, many teachers in Cuban schools approach children with the same tired methods used in boring classrooms throughout the world." [21] One observer, upon entering a lactante playroom, noticed a girl, about a year old, alone in a play- pen with only a large, heavy ball to play with. The child could hardly move it. With no other toy available, the baby finally gave up on the ball and sat staring off into space.[22] Why a year-old baby was given only one heavy object to play with and why no one thought to interest the child in other activities is, of course, the question that comes to mind. Instructions from above explicitly state that all círculo workers are to make sure that nursing babies receive the proper attention, and that those who work with these infants design and make their own toys for the children to play with if there are no factory-made playthings available. Everyone "should cooperate in the all-important task of gathering materials for the toys, so indispensable to the nursery." [23]

Lactante equipment is generally well-built and sturdy, providing opportunity for large-muscle play (such as crawling in and out of the circular holes of the floor playpen) and contact with other children in safe areas (as in the corral and at the feeding tables). Most equipment either is acquired directly from Eastern Europe under special trade arrangements or is copied from Eastern European and other models. Most lactante rooms have floor playpens, but no special corrals, although I also noted rooms with corrals, but no playpens. Swings were to be found in most círculos, yet in the círculo I describe here, there was none.

Others who have visited lactante rooms report on the lack of toys, mobiles, and other colorful and interesting objects in the rooms or cribs. Garrity, reporting on her 1970 trip, laments, "The walls were basically bare. One infant room did have a large plastic doll hanging from the ceiling over a playpen. Children were given toys in the playpens, but the toys often seemed inappropriate—no soft toys, no rattles, only rubber squeeze toys. . . . The atmosphere and the amount of materials was very similar" in all of the círculos Garrity visited. "None of the centers had many toys. There were usually a half dozen rubber squeeze dolls, some plastic toys or cars, a book or two, some wooden climbing apparatus for the smallest children, and something additional in each place." Noteworthy, however, is the fact that "Oftentimes the toys were out of the reach of children." [24]

On the day I visited the círculo here described—and on

following days—I noted a ratio of four staff members to eleven children; the official registration of the group was seventeen. The ratio naturally fluctuated depending on staff problems, sickness, and other factors. From what I gathered, the ratio varies from círculo to círculo (the official ratio is one to ten). There were six staff members assigned to this room and they maintained the following hours:

1 lactante *responsable*	9 A.M.–5 P.M.
1 asistente	6 A.M.–2 P.M.
2 asistentes (split shift)	7 A.M.–12 noon;
	4 P.M.–7 P.M.
2 asistentes	9 A.M.–5 P.M.
1 asistente	11 A.M.–7 P.M.

Of the six staff members scheduled to work in the room— not counting the *responsable* (the working supervisor)— four were usually there at any one time.

Parvulitos (Toddlers)

Once the visitor has accustomed himself to seeing infants in a day-care setting, visiting the toddlers comes perfectly naturally. Often parvulitos are divided into two sub-groups with the fourteen-to-eighteen-month-old children in one and the eighteen-to-twenty-four-month-old children in another. The division depends upon the size of the group in a given círculo.

In the group described here four asistentes work these shifts, or *turnos:*

asistente 1	6 A.M.–2 P.M.
asistente 2	9 A.M.–5 P.M.
asistente 3 (split shift)	7 A.M.–11 A.M.
	3 P.M.–6 P.M.
asistente 4	11 A.M.–7 P.M.

For the approximately fifty children in this group, the ratio was one asistente to ten youngsters. In the early and late hours of the day, the staff was smaller.

In the early morning, after breakfast, the children had their clothes changed and played outdoors. While those who had already been changed waited for the others to get ready, they played with little rectangular cars in a large, spacious room.

On the patio, the children and an asistente played such games as "open-shut them" (opening and closing the fingers of both hands while they sing "open-shut them") in small circles. Until juice time, they took turns on the slide or played ball. Cups were soon brought out on the patio and each child was called by name for his juice. Afterward, sitting in a circle, the children sang songs, while small groups were taken to be bathed. After a while an asistente suggested, "Let's go to the shade." She led the children out of the hot sun and took them to a cool, shady spot.

Bath time was happy, friendly, and fun. Lázara, one of the smaller children in the group, greatly enjoyed it. She and the other children happily took their baths in a tile tub. While bathing them, the asistentes kept up a constant chatter. One exclaimed, "¡Qué rico!" and made other comments to each child. This one's hair was getting longer, a bruise on another child's face seemed better. After drying, the children were powdered with talcum, and then took naps on small cots, their sneakers on the floor beneath them. Asistentes continued to bathe the children by twos and then took them to their cots.

Lázara would not sleep; she got off her cot and moved a few steps. An asistente scolded, "¡Lázara!," picked her up and put her back on her cot. With a twinkle in her eye, Lázara got out of bed again and raised one hand as if she were performing calisthenics. Again, the asistente reprimanded her, and she finally settled back on her cot and played with her toes. A minute or two afterward, she fell asleep.

While the younger ones were napping, the older children collected grass, acorns, and leaves at a nearby beach. "Let's go to the beach to gather different things," an asistente had coaxed. I noticed a boy taunting a girl by waving grass in her face, and she responded by banging him on the head with a pail. At first he made a low noise that seemed as if it would become a loud howl. But the noise stopped as suddenly as it began, and he walked off, distracted, picking up other things. Apparently feeling that this activity had not caught on very well, at 11:05 A.M. two asistentes led the group back indoors.

Inside, the adults sat down on the floor with the children as they played with small, colored blocks which fit into wooden cars. As the children, obviously accustomed to these blocks, played, the teachers built their own little block projects, playing in parallel with the children; sometimes an asistente would turn to a child who had asked a question; some youngsters used the toy-car holders as part of their creations; one little girl piled up four blocks and proudly exclaimed, "Hurrah!" and an asistente happily turned to her, repeating, "Hurrah!" A boy, Andrés, placed spool-like cylinders one on top of another, adding three blocks to the spools. A girl, who noticed the tall structure, added two more blocks. She sighed, "¡Ay!" as it all toppled. The original engineer laughed and both children spiritedly reconstructed the tower. After a while the girl walked off and Andrés, with legs extended "V" style, played alone. Finally he knocked the spools down himself. With a signal of "¡Vamos!" from one of the asistentes, the children put the blocks into little wagons and piled them against the wall.

Meanwhile, at about 11:15, Lázara woke up, crying. An asistente consoled her, bringing her blue sneakers.

Soon after, kitchen helpers wheeled in an aluminum

wagon with four-compartment metal trays. A large section of the tray offered a macaroni mixture with meat and cheese. Each child had a large and a small spoon set at his place at the table and they all served themselves. Lázara gobbled up her food with a large spoon, uninterested in the three other children at her table. No one talked.

As Lázara finished, another child, at a neighboring table, made a bowel movement. An asistente cleaned it up matter-of-factly with toilet paper; no fuss was made. As she poured a pail of water over the marble floor, the three other children at Lázara's table continued eating. A boy seated next to Lázara offered her a spoonful of food from his plate. "No!" she responded. The boy then turned to his right, offering the same spoonful to another child.

At 11:35, another worker joined the staff, thirty-five minutes late. Her shift started at eleven o'clock, but I later learned than she had had an appointment with her doctor. This asistente was quite proud of Lázara—because, she noted, Lázara always "eats up everything." Pointing to a boy in the group, she observed disapprovingly, "He doesn't like macaroni." She then went to where Lázara was seated and wiped her mouth with toilet paper.

Shortly thereafter, when almost all of the children had finished their meal, flan—a custard—was served in little dishes, along with milk in metal cups. Evaporated milk was served to those who did not drink regular milk. Suddenly, Lázara spilled her milk and an asistente, while wiping it up with that ubiquitous círculo equipment—toilet paper—reprimanded the little girl, "Lázara, Lázara, please!" At one point, Lázara tried to take off her bib by herself. She worked diligently with her hands behind her back. Finally, she turned it around, managing the task with a triumphant sigh.

Others have observed situations that reflect much the

same atmosphere as does this parvulito group. Garrity reports that in one círculo, during free play on the patio, two tricycles and three or four small toys were brought out for eight children.[25] Those with the toys sat holding them or talked to themselves quietly. The youngsters with the tricycles did not peddle but rather pushed them from behind like stalled automobiles. Children without toys sat and stared. The day-care workers on duty stood at the door, which enabled them to observe both the children playing outdoors and the others napping inside. "I did not see a child try to go inside (after more toys) or try to take a toy from another child."

Garrity notes, however, that "by far the most predominant activity" in the Cuban day-care centers is the circle game.[26] Conducted by an adult, either indoors or out, these games can have as many as fifteen to twenty children participating. Garrity witnessed several circle games and indicated that the younger children had a difficult time concentrating on this form of play. At one círculo, eleven children with their asistente were in a circle in a field. While the day-care worker tried to lead the children in a song, the latter were continually distracted by a group of older children across the field. Even after the asistente adjusted the seating arrangements to allow more children into the circle in order to hold their attention, the youngsters failed to respond; their interest in the activities across the field never flagged.

In another center Garrity watched four or five circle games going on simultaneously. With a day-care worker in the center of each, other asistentes stood at the side, uninvolved. Some circles were playing exercise games while others were singing or bouncing balls. Inasmuch as most of the children were just learning how to bounce balls, the game was slow and tedious. Finally, the asistentes gave up instructing and relied only on those children who knew how to bounce the ball back and forth. Those who did not participate fidgeted or stared off into the distance. Garrity summed up:

A Cuban circle game often appears analogous to a group activity in the U.S. where children work in rows. However, what particularly struck me in the Cuban activities was the lack of involvement by all but a few children. In each circle game there were always sev-

Table 8: Daily Parvulito Schedule *(14 Months–2 Years)*		
	Time	*Activity*
A.M.	6:30–7:30	arrival
	7:30–8:00	breakfast
	8:00–8:30	clean-up
	8:30–10:30	outdoor activities
	10:30–11:30	bath; nap for 18-month-olds
	11:30–12:30 P.M.	lunch
P.M.	12:30–2:30	nap for those over 18 months
	2:00–2:30	bath for those under 18 months
	2:30–4:00	outdoor activities (over 18 months)
	4:00–5:00	dinner
	5:00–7:00	change clothes; free games outdoors
	7:30–8:30	milk at home

eral children staring blankly, and many other children sitting or standing listlessly observing. Children I have observed in the U.S., when not involved in a group activity, often act out by squirming, hitting another child, or fiddling with something. It was my impression that the uninvolved Cuban children were quiet, passive, non-aggressive, not acting out. The contrast to what I was used to in American children in similar situations was striking.[27]

Activities for the parvulitos and older groups are listed on bulletin boards in every day-care center in Cuba. Tables

Table 9: Daily Párvulos Schedule (2–4 Years)		
	Time	*Activity*
A.M.	6:30–7:30	arrival
	7:30–8:00	breakfast
	8:00–8:30	toilet; wash hands
	8:30–10:30	outdoor activities
	10:30–11:30	bath
	11:30–12:30	lunch
P.M.	12:30–2:30	nap
	2:30–4:00	cleanup and free games
	4:00–5:00	dinner
	5:00–7:00	change clothes; outdoor activities
	7:30–8:30	milk at home

8–10 [28] present the prescribed schedule for parvulitos, párvulos, and pre-escolares.

Karen's Diary

Official visitors who tour educational facilities often observe situations and settings that may not represent common practice, frequently seeing only model classrooms and particularly successful schools. Under these conditions, it is impossible to judge the routine classroom. Those who re-

---

Table 10: Daily Pre-Escolar Schedule (4–5 Years)

	Time	Activity
A.M.	6:00–7:30	arrival
	7:30–8:00	breakfast
	8:00–11:00	educational activities with kindergarten teacher
	9:30–10:00	snack
	11:00–noon	bath
P.M.	noon–12:30	lunch
	1:00–2:30	nap
	2:30–4:30	outdoor activities (free and planned)
	4:30–5:30	dinner
	5:30–7:00	activities and change of clothes
	8:00–9:00	milk at home

turn from guided tours are correctly asked by their colleagues whether or not the reports they bring back are meaningful in terms of the nation or whether what they saw was an isolated display, that is not indicative of the system as a whole. Those who do not have a chance to wander and observe without official guidance must honestly report that the sites visited may not be representative; in fact, they may be unique.

My own observations of Cuban schools are based on visits to círculos over many consecutive days. Although my experiences were not those of the one-shot, "official" variety, I was nevertheless a visitor, with all that that implies. As it happened, my fourteen-year old daughter, who accompanied me during my stay in Cuba, worked as a volunteer asistente in a Cuban day-care center; luckily, she kept a diary of her experiences and it is instructive to read her notes and compare them with some of the observations I have already reported. Since Karen was part of the círculo team, she was able to see from "within" what others, including myself, could only guess at as outsiders.

The following excerpt from her diary illustrates, among other things, that brief visits may not reflect the norm. This passage also gives a telling insider's glimpse of the use—or misuse—of toys and materials; it makes clear that even when equipment is not in short supply, it might as well not exist at all if the center ignores it.

This morning when I arrived, it was pretty late. Most of the kids had arrived; most were dressed and in their school clothes and were in the back room where we stay. The boys have little shorts, and they keep their own shoes and shorts. It is not a uniform; all different shorts and all different dresses are used for them to play in. It was comparatively silent and they were all sitting in a circle.

The assistant then told me that visitors were coming today. So I assumed that they were waiting for them to come and they were going to be "very good." They were Japanese visitors and the visitors were already outside, near the director's office.

We got them into a "good" circle and an asistente said, "Listen, I want you all to be very good and I want you all to sing your best. If you sing well, I'll give you *caramelos.*"

In her own way she was urging them, with this bribe, to sing well. It was a straight-out reward. "Remember, when they come in we will sing a cheer for them." Finally, the Japanese visitors came in and the children cheered.

A Japanese woman had a camera and took some pictures. Outside, in the back, the children were sitting in three circles, the parvulitos and párvulos and the pre-escolares. They sang for the visitors and they did really sing well.

Finally, the visitors left and one girl, who had done something wrong, was told by the asistente that she would not get a caramelo. The asistente was angry at her and very rough. The director came by, noted what was happening, and said firmly, "Don't do that to her."

One thing I noticed was that asistentes were always being very physical with the kids, hugging them, touching them, whether it was for love or punishment.

I was surprised to see so many visitors that day—in addition to the Japanese about forty French people had come. I was told that every Friday there were visitors. One Friday a truckload of Russians arrived. Then a small group of French young people came. They were interested in our songs, but they were really more interested in taking pictures—especially of a very dark-skinned boy; they loved him and played with him. They didn't pay much attention to the asistentes or any other staff. They talked to the director for a while and afterward came back to us.

For the first time since I had been there they gave out toys for the children to play with. They gave out small colored blocks, with ABC's; the kids were so unaccustomed to these blocks that I never saw such an uproar. The kids were just not used to having such an abundance of toys. It could have been the disorganization; there was enough for everybody, but when they put them out, everybody scrambled for them.

I could not believe that they had had these blocks and toys and had not given them out every day. Each batch of blocks was in a box with wheels, different colored blocks, with ABC's; there were a few balls, a few little miniature bowling pins in different colors, a few broken dolls—not just the good dolls that were on display. I'm sure it looked nice to the visitors to see a lot of toys. They took pictures. Finally they left and we put the toys away.

What happens when children arrive at school often indicates their feelings about it. In the United States, for example, I have frequently seen children dawdling in the yard or straggling to school as limp and tired as if they had just finished heavy labor. The chore of taking those last steps through the school door has so exhausted them that no energy seems to be left to face the pain of the classroom. I have also witnessed children dashing from the school bus into school.

At more than twenty círculos that I observed, I saw very little resistance or objection from the youngsters as they were left off by their parents. For the most part, friendly parent good-bys were exchanged for warm welcomes from the asistentes. Karen describes a morning scene:

I came in early and parents were dropping off the kids and I was watching to see the kids' reactions as they left their parents. Most just walked right in as if it were their home, very happy that they were there. Only about three—out of all those I saw—were crying. One was in my group and I tried to comfort her. She wanted her mother but she also wanted her pacifier; I guess the asistentes really wanted the children to stop the habit of sucking on a pacifier so they did not give it to her. This made the girl more hysterical. She didn't want anyone to touch her. The asistente didn't just let her cry, she tried to get her to join the other children. She told me to leave her alone because the girl only wanted the pacifier. . . . After some time the little girl got over it.

Garrity's observations at two different círculos demonstrate that the tone and attitude of the personnel at different day-care centers can be enormously different; in one, leave-taking in the evening can be painful, while in another it can be pleasant.[29] At one center, there was no effective transition from the asistentes to the family, while at another, a casual change-over was encouraged. At still another center, parents were made to wait outside while the asistentes readied the children for home, yet at another, parents were invited into the children's rooms and could stay as long as they wished.

At Karen's círculo, the "Monday syndrome" infected everyone. Karen reports how difficult it was to console the children:

Monday mornings were really hard on all of us because the kids had just spent the weekend with their families. Even the *internados* [boarding students] had spent Sunday and part of Saturday with their parents. They had all just gotten adjusted to being home again and now were very sad to leave their parents. In my group there were very few who came without crying, without separation worries, without mothers saying, "Wait, I'll get you this or that. Don't cry." They cried for a very long time after they were separated from their mothers, and it was very hard for us to control them. I went upstairs and there was a little girl going, "Mommy, mommy." It must have been really hard for her.

Then they dressed them and I helped. Afterward, we went downstairs where the children were having free play. They were still crying and I remember that the asistentes handled the crying by completely ignoring it. They didn't hold them; they just let them cry it out. "They'll get over it," and that's it. They didn't pick any of the kids up when they were crying. I did; but the others just ignored them. Sometimes they would even say, "Stop crying." Their way of handling it was not to do anything but to let them cry it out.

That this situation was handled in this manner is probably more a reflection of the level of competence of this particular staff than of the spirit of the círculos. What the Cuban leadership says about adaptation to the círculo environment is pertinent here:

The success or failure in the adaptation of the child to the círculo depends on whether or not his stay there is happy. For this reason we must give maximum attention to new arrivals and attend to each case according to its circumstances. But the child-care assistant must, in all cases, give the child love and attention, thereby establishing an indispensable affective relationship between herself and the child.[30]

In an account from Karen's diary dated July 28, 1969, we learn of the place the círculo has in the lives of the asistentes, even when they are officially off-duty. Karen reiterates what we have already reported on the lack of adequate materials, particularly picture books for the little children.

There are these two kids, brother and sister; the sister is a little younger and they came very late one day. But everyone loved these two—they are the favorites of the whole school. Everybody hugged and kissed them, and then, later in the day, when I was starting to tell them a story, the little boy came over to me and he said, "Did you see my little sister?" He was so proud when he said that. I said, "Is she in the parvulitos?" He said, "Yes" and nodded his head, and stood so proud. It was great to see so close a relationship between brother and sister.

I had taken a little book along called *Buddy Bones* about two brothers who had toys and never took care of them. I don't think they really got everything in the story. It was just nice having a story being read to them, and they all crowded around and listened to it. I asked them questions. The level of the book was too hard for them; they needed a book with more pictures and fewer words. I tried to simplify it as I went along and I skipped around; I didn't read the book page by page. They got a little of it and they liked to see the pictures, but it was really the whole idea of telling a story that they liked. While I was telling the story, Vicky and the other asistente gave out lemonade. They gave some to me, too.

Sonja, another asistente, came to the círculo in the afternoon to help Vicky. Since she usually worked mornings, it seemed she was there because she had nothing else to do so she came to see the kids. Later on, sometime after the lemonade, we all got water.

Another diary entry calls attention to the problems faced by asistentes in dealing with the heavy routines while at the same time offering more than custodial care to the children. Karen describes a morning activity in the círculo in which an asistente handles a problem rather nicely:

In the morning they were singing in circles and they had pails and played "at the beach." At about eleven o'clock they started to take four children out at a time to bathe while the others finished collecting rocks in their pails. The asistente called them together, and took them around a big tub of water. They had a little water activity—observing a boat in the water and pushing it, playing with it. Then they rested and talked and sang, and meanwhile they kept on taking four in and four out until they were ready for lunch. One asistente was bathing them and another helping, while the other two were sort of supervising the beach activity.

I focused on one kid, Ana, and I watched what happened to her. Ana was sometimes with the group; sometimes she wandered away. I took some notes on what she was doing. She became very fascinated with the beach activity. She was picking up little seeds—like pine cones—from the pine trees, and filling her pail with pine leaves and acorns. She was fascinated and completely involved. At one point, she got into a little difficulty because somebody emptied the pail. She got upset and cried. An asistente came over and asked what had happened. Ana told her it was "all thrown out." The asistente said, "Pick it up." This seemed to satisfy her. Then they collected all the pails. Yet Ana was still upset because now she didn't want her pail to be taken away. The asistente looked at her and let her keep the pail while they went on to the next activity. Ana was holding on to the pail and another child wanted it also. He went over and started to push her while trying to take the pail. The asistente took the pail from the two of them and told Ana she would play with it tomorrow. Ana accepted that. She put her thumb into her mouth every once in a while to comfort herself.

The problem of bathing routines, the shortage of asistentes, and attitudes toward other activities are reflected in excerpts concerning Karen's first day in the círculo. Inasmuch as bathing is a basic part of the círculo program, the result is often that the mere physical demands make it very difficult for workers to switch to an open, "free" attitude about the children getting dirty. Karen's reaction, while influenced by her youth and the novelty of the situation, nevertheless reflects the feeling of asistentes with whom I have spoken. At a collective of provincial leaders of the círculos which I attended, there was common agreement that asistentes throughout the country had been told many times about the importance of permitting the children to play with toys and materials, of even letting them "mess up." However, the local leadership said that time and again on visits to the círculos they would find the toys in a closet because of the problem of clean-up chores or the asistentes' desire for clean floors. Thus, Karen's reaction to the messiness reflects the círculo asistente's reaction after she has just spent a whole morning bathing the children.

When I got there there were two teachers preparing the kids who slept in the círculo. There were many kids and they were busy getting them up and getting them dressed. She showed me the place where they kept their pajamas, sort of a community thing where they kept special clothes and everyday clothes. They had one drawer for all the pajamas, and a bag for the dirty laundry.

They don't call the workers teachers, because they only have a sixth-grade education. She is called "asistente." When I said I was in the eighth grade she said, "Wow!" They gave me one of the jobs of bathing the children. The kids were playing by themselves. One asistente was absent and so they asked me to take her place. The job was to take off the kids' clothes and when they finished bathing to dress them again.

There was another asistente bathing the children who really was great with kids. We went upstairs to where there was a shower, but they didn't use the shower, they used a big tub of water and she used a wash cloth with soap, pouring water over them. It must have been freezing water because the heater wasn't working that day. The kids got very nervous but the asistente said that it didn't matter. A few kids were crying, afraid to go in. I was sort of surprised because I thought they were used to bathing every day. Maybe they were not used to the cold water. I started to take off the girls' shoes and their underpants and dresses. The boys have pants without underpants which made it easier and I would put the clothes under a seat. Four at a time they would come up. The asistente would bathe them and the children would come to me and I would put their clothes on again. Four would come up, four would go down, and we spent all morning bathing them. It was really a big project.

Afterward I went down to the dining room and I found them all seated at tables for lunch. Finally, the lunch came, served on trays. All the kids eat at the same time. These are parvulitos, two- and three-year-olds. We set the trays on the tables. Most of them ate by themselves and they were only two and three years old! If they didn't eat by themselves they waited for someone to come over and feed them. They were very messy and I thought, "Oh, gee, after all that bathing and now they are messy again." One boy was completely covered with his soup. I can't describe how messy it was.

Some of the asistentes made the kids eat all the food. One boy was crying because he didn't want to eat it all. I just couldn't make anybody eat everything.

The asistentes left the kids at the table while they went to set up for nap time. The kids started fooling around with the water, splashing, joking. They really were having a ball. I thought this was great and the asistente didn't seem to worry, which was sort of un-Cuban, not being worried about clean, clean, clean, beautifully clean. It was like a finger-paint scene— only using water.

After lunch we went out. They took a wash cloth and went over each kid because they were really dirty. They set up cots—which were just big enough for them—wooden frames with white canvas. What was interesting was that one of the asistentes, the one who seemed to yell a lot, was "throwing" the kids around; what was amazing to me was that in spite of her rough manner she really was a soft person and I think the kids feel it. She really is very friendly. They all like her and come to her.

The kids got on the cots. We went around helping them take off their shoes and put them under the cots. The asistente said, "Today everybody is going to sleep." Only about two or three didn't sleep, but they rested quietly instead. They all seemed to be used to the routine of taking the nap. When they got onto their cots, the asistentes and I would sit by each child who couldn't sleep. We would pat them, hum to them, or just sit by their side.

Directed Learning

In their attempt to transform a backward educational system into a modern, thriving teaching and learning force, one might have thought that Cuban educators would, by fiat, deny the "bourgeois" past and begin their system by ignoring history. On the contrary, Cubans, rather than denying traditional Western educational philosophy, have found these sources quite fruitful.

Since the intelligentsia in pre-revolutionary Cuba drew many of its theories and ideas from the U. S. and European experience, it is not surprising to find some Cuban scholars who have been trained in universities and colleges in the United States and Western Europe. Even today, many students and educators benefit from training abroad. With little native tradition in early-childhood education, Cuban educators, administrators, and psychologists have chosen the eclectic route: snipping this scholar for a key to early-childhood development, turning to that psychologist for a clue to the learning process, manipulating a theory, transforming a concept, grappling, groping, coping.

Partly because of the U. S. embargo of Cuba—which makes receipt of U. S. educational materials a difficult and time-consuming task—and partly because of the serious shortage of native Cuban educational and psychological personnel, there appears to be little knowledge about the most recent U. S. developments in early-childhood education. However, in my conversations with young Cuban psychologists who assist the círculo leadership, I noted that they were quite well aware of the work of Jean Piaget, L. S. Vygotsky, and others.

Figure 1, from Cuban psychiatrist J. Pérez Villar's text used for in-service training, shows two of the classical Piaget experiments with water levels and conservation of quantity.[31] An inspection of Pérez's twenty-seven-item bibliography reveals that, except for a single reference to Soviet psychologist R. N. Leontiev's work, and aside from two references to Cuban material, all the rest of the sources are from U.S. and Western European research. Among the authors cited by Pérez are Erik Erikson, Arnold Gessel, both Anna and Sigmund Freud, and Margaret Mead. Almost a third of the references are devoted to Piaget's work.

It should also be noted that in the United States and elsewhere, early-childhood educational studies have recently focused on the three- to four-year-old children, while the círculos have plunged ahead and developed curricula for children as young as forty-five days old.

The Cubans have not ignored Marxist experience and theory, but they have not restricted themselves to pure Marxist conceptions. No theory, no school, no expert is

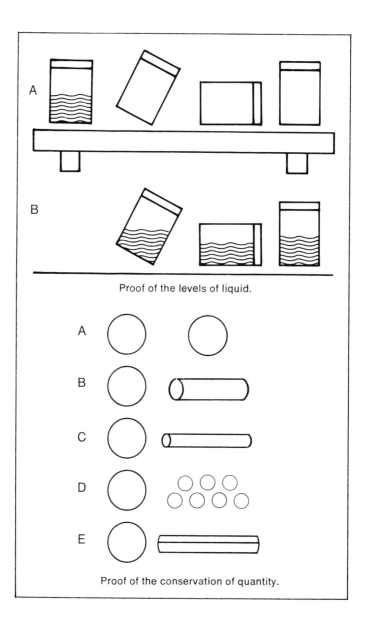

Proof of the levels of liquid.

Proof of the conservation of quantity.

chosen as the sole arbiter of educational thought. The child and the future of Cuba are the two values uppermost in their minds. "If it works, use it" seems to be the general rule prevailing.

Leading psychologists in the Ministry of Education wholly reject complete obeisance to the Soviet school. One psychologist commented: "In the development of psychology in the Soviet Union there was sometimes an exaggerated, rather mechanical, adherence to psychophysiology. It was easier, far more comfortable, always to resort to the conditioned reflex." [32]

Directed learning—as opposed to a freer, "spontaneous" approach—is the system used in the círculos. Childhood development is seen as a ladder, with each age group comprising another rung toward adulthood. Highly structured, círculo activities correspond to the separate steps children must take. Recognizing that the development of logical thought is a primary aim of intellectual growth, the círculo programs follow strict developmental schemes so that children will master skills in a step-by-step, orderly fashion. Echoing Jerome Bruner, Miranda remarked, "We believe that the child's education can be directed, though not inflexibly or rigidly. What we mean by this is: what thing or activity can favor a given aspect of development in a child? We then provide that activity. Our education is 'directed,' therefore, in the sense of a planned end. Children can be taught anything if we know how to teach it to them in a form that they are able to assimilate." [33]

Círculo educators subscribe to the views of many U. S. psychologists, including Jacob Gerwitz, Martin Deutsch, and Sally Provence, who believe that by controlling childhood experience one can profoundly affect intellectual growth. According to these thinkers, the preschool environment is not merely an environment wherein a set of conditions acts on the child to elicit certain behavior, but is a plastic medium, one that flows in both directions: children elicit various responses, and, simultaneously, respond selectively to stimuli in order to gratify their needs. The intensity of these experiences depends, in large measure, on the child's stage·of development. For Provence, it is important that the environment be stocked with variety and contrast, so that the child receives both stimulation and protection.[34] In that environment most conducive to learning, the child should be free from major discomfort and painful stimuli. The atmosphere must also allow for perceptive skill development and the creation of mild states of tension calling for adaptive response. Piaget suggests that the child's world must provide stimuli varying in number and dimension; otherwise, the evocative power of the environment will be lost and the child will "die" of educational boredom.[35]

In the 1960s, directed learning in early-childhood education was stressed in a number of programs and studies. J. McVicker Hunt, Martin Deutsch, Carl Bereiter, David Weikert, and others [36] in the United States strongly encouraged the creation of preschool activities that provide a host of specific experiences to create a more keenly aware child. Writing about his work at the Institute of Developmental Studies, Deutsch concluded:

We have emphasized the role of specific social attributes and experiences in the development of language and verbal behavior, of concept formation and organization, of visual and auditory discrimination, of general environmental orientation, and of self-concepts and motivation . . . and all this to school performance. . . . A compensatory program for children, starting at three or four years of age, might provide the maximum of opportunity for prevention of future disabilities and for remediation of current skill deficiencies. In addition, such a program might serve to minimize the effect of discontinuity between home and school environment, thereby enhancing the child's functional adjustment to school requirements.[37]

The principles of directed learning in early-childhood education are translated to the círculo through the training of its leaders as well as through programs based on these principles. In 1969, I attended a seminar of círculo leaders from all the provinces of Cuba. Most of those who attended had never heard the name of Piaget before, yet under the guidance of a twenty-six-year-old psychologist from the Ministry of Education, they were studying the various stages of child development as outlined by Piaget. After class, they visited various nursery schools. Upon returning to the seminar, they described the behavior they had observed with special focus on children's play at different ages. These leaders were expected to organize similar seminars in their own provinces.

The círculo, according to Cuban thought, should present activities that will enable children to acquire skills and develop modes of learning appropriate at their age level. In essence, the círculo program attempts to provide what U.S psychologist J. McVicker Hunt calls "the proper match" between the child's developmental level and the materials and activities provided. The rungs of development provide a fixed system: each normal child takes the same steps at about the same rate. Educators do not believe in letting children hang back or climb the ladder at their own speed. The steps must be taken at appropriate moments, and it is the duty of the círculos to accelerate the learning process by directing children toward the skills corresponding to their level of maturation. Cuban educators feel that the child must be stimulated at exactly the right point in his development so that he can successfully complete one stage and go on immediately to the next.

Emphasizing that directed activity means giving "directions" to the leader, who is the "arranger" of the environment, and not the programer of the child, Clementina Serra emphasized that Cubans do not want to wait for the results of maturation: the círculo hopes to take a more vigorous course.[38]

The asistente is critical to the success of directed learning, and must have a fairly good idea of when children are ready to respond to given stimuli. She must adroitly manipulate the child's activity, understanding the relation of stimulation to capacity at a particular stage in his intellectual development. Shaping the child's environment, the asistente must be careful to promote the desired accumulation of motor, social, and cognitive skills at just the right time. As a good baker knows the right moment to take the bread from the oven, so a good asistente knows exactly when a child is ready to receive a given piece of information, or to accept the challenge of acquiring a certain skill. If directed learning is handled correctly, the child will learn to establish personal controls and to increase the range of alternative behavior capable of coping with varied situations.

Deutsch suggests that by structuring the child's esperiences with an emphasis on verbal interaction, the day-care worker can aid in the child's acquisition of appropriate speech patterns.[39] Inasmuch as speech is an internal process learned from others, the asistente should engage the child in real dialogues, promoting the development of his speech. As language ability increases, so does the capacity for logical thought.

The basic curriculum of the círculos reflects several fundamental tenets of childhood development and its concomitant educational process. A report on the Círculos Infantiles by Clementina Serra relates Cuban theory on the schools' role in this development.

The development of the physical as well as the sociological function of children is constant. All of the changes which occur during that process are products of two basic factors which act reciprocally upon each other: maturation and learning. This means, from the educational point of view, that for proper development it is not sufficient to wait for the result of maturation, it is not sufficient to wait for the development of the organism which should and will come as a result of time. We must unite experience to maturation—this is what we mean by learning.

Thus, it is necessary to encourage and direct multiple learning corresponding to different age groups at that moment when the processes of maturation permit them. At such times the child is ready to acquire new experiences. . . .

Within these age groups handled by the Círculos Infantiles, learning must take place in a spontaneous manner and not under the discipline of older children. In these years, learning is realized by provoking the capabilities and abilities developing in the child at his level of maturation. To achieve these results it is enough to present children with stimuli which we already know will cause them to act in a predetermined way. . . .

"Programmed or directed activities" should not be interpreted to mean to coercively impose formal activities on the children. When we place a toy or a brilliant object in front of a child in the crawling area we know beforehand what his reaction will be: he will move to reach it. This is precisely what we wish: we want the child to crawl, to practice a new activity, and he does. From the asistente's point of view, we call this process directed activity, although the conduct of the child who has moved (not as the result of an order, but in answer to a determined situation) is spontaneous.[40]

According to Serra, logical thought processes are the highest form of human activity and therefore ought to be guided and strongly encouraged. The child's perceptive, memory, and language skills are indispensable to thought. In theory, children ought to be placed in the midst of "sonorous, mobile toys which they can clutch, suck on, and push" to acquaint them with their surrounding environment and refine their perceptive abilities.

Directed learning programs in the círculos cover all aspects of the child's physical, mental, and emotional development, with the greatest attention given to the four- and five-year-olds. At their inception, the círculos had set weekly plans that lacked activities aimed toward specific learning goals. Marta Santander regrets not having given more difficult tasks to younger children in the early days. "We had never thought to present the younger children with something difficult, like teaching them a complete song. It didn't occur to us." Now that the developmental learning program is structured and more formalized, the círculos have instituted a series of games, puzzles, and other materials "to help the child develop his thinking power, his powers of analysis." [41]

Asistentes must understand the child's developmental stages so that they can appropriately guide his learning. Santander noted muscular control as a case in point:

Muscular control is involved in climbing stairs, walking down a ramp, crawling under a rope, picking up blocks and putting them in a container, running. What age group is each game for? Teachers must know when each group is ready for a specific toy or game, what difficulties the children will have with that particular game or toy, and how much attention the instructor should give the children. And if there are some children who have more difficulties, then we must see whether the child has a physical problem or whether the teacher should devote a bit more time to that child.

A reading of círculo plans and programs reveals a detailed and structured set of routines designed to develop many skills, from the control of equilibrium in four-year-olds (by having them walk frontward and sideways along a plank raised twenty to fifty centimeters from the floor) to the acquisition of appropriate patriotic responses through discussions on the life of Che, "who was very brave and who, after helping the Cubans, went to help another country." [42] Although the plans are fairly detailed, círculo educators point out that these are merely guidelines which círculo personnel complete at their own discretion. As Santander notes:

Whenever an opportunity arises the alert teacher takes advantage of it to broaden the children's experience. The structure we provide suggests that in a specific lesson, pictures or posters would be best to illustrate a point. The plan provides a general outline. The teachers have great flexibility in applying the plans.[43]

She gave a specific example:

In the week that we had planned to tell the children about letters and mailmen, I arrived at the nursery just as the mailman was arriving. I asked him to come in with me so that the children could see him and his mail bag. It would go so well with the lesson. But he said he was tired, and besides he was in a hurry. I promised him he could have some cold water, coffee perhaps, and at least take the weight off his feet and rest a few minutes, so he agreed to come in. Well, the children were delighted! They crawled all over him, and he really enjoyed it. He began taking letters out of the bag and showing them all to the children, and answering questions. He just loved it! It was a wonderful lesson. You should never force an explanation on children simply because it's planned. If it doesn't seem like the right time, do it another time. But this worked out just beautifully. Things have to be presented in a natural, relaxed manner, and that's not easy.[44]

Directed learning in Cuban day-care centers goes quite far. For example, experiments with teaching five-year-olds to read and write began in September 1971. "We know that those who learned to read and write at five years old show absolutely no difference from the others in any respect—in gaiety, movements, interests, or anything else," reports Miranda.[45] Encouraged by the results of their early reading program designed for five-year-olds, the círculos experimented with reading and writing for four-year-olds. The plans call for close observation of the children followed by studies that seek for any signs of psychological damage; Miranda indicated that if the new program affects children adversely, they will abandon it. Conducted over a three-year period, experiments with five-year-old children showed that 92 percent of the more than five hundred children in the pilot project learned to read and write in four months.[46] The círculos note that many of those who did not succeed had failed to attend class for one reason or another. Particularly proud of the fact that the experiment in reading and writing with the five-year-olds was conducted by regular asistentes, the círculos also point out that the children, too, were drawn from normal classes; no special selection was made of either the teachers or the children in any of the thirty pilot projects. Miranda enthusiastically recalls, "Just as soon as the children had learned to read their first few words, they begged the asistentes to teach them more." [47]

There has been a debate over teaching young children to read and write that has not yet ended. The círculos seem headed in a direction that calls for their children to learn to read and write earlier and earlier. No clear case has been made to prove that scholastic achievement of young children is essential for any reason. What does it matter that children can read and write at a given set of signals rather than salivate at the ringing of a bell? The círculos must ask themselves: What ultimate good is derived from teaching children to read before they are ready to understand?

Formal reading and writing on a wide scale is not yet

taught in Cuban day-care centers, however. In general, the current goal is to prepare children to begin learning these skills in the first grade.

Early-childhood educators are exposed to several sources of curriculum guidance and information, which are also used as key curriculum resources in the brief three-month training program as well as in ongoing in-service training. One source is an educational periodical called *Simientes*. The other sources are the syllabus or *plan de trabajo* and the *planeamientos*.

Simientes, a "how to" magazine, is published every month. The only regularly published source of materials and aids for Cuban early-childhood programs, *Simientes* has sent a steady flow of pedagogical materials into classrooms for the past five years. Each issue usually includes a fairly easy-to-understand psychopedagogical article which is the basis for in-service training study circle discussions in the círculos themselves. *Simientes* also includes rhymes, songs (including the music), stories, riddles, instructions for creating puppets, and art aids. Although some of the covers of *Simientes* freely use color and contemporary design, the accent in the journal itself is on sample cut-outs, or coloring-in line drawings. Almost every issue offers an idea for children's theater, with suggested scripts filled with animal characters; ideas for pantomime, puppetry, acting-out are suggested. Early issues excerpted articles from Soviet journals on child development; but recent ones consist of articles written for asistentes by the círculo leadership (usually Dr. Miranda).

As critics of the school of directed learning have pointed out, it is open to serious question whether strict allegiance to stimulation along definite developmental lines is best for the child as a total human being. In other words, does directed learning limit the child's creativity and initiative?

Burton L. White argues that if we indeed believe that cognitive development is enough, then those techniques that strengthen the child's skills in mathematics, language, and reading are all that is required.[48]

If one of the chief goals of Cuban preschool education is the creation of the new Cuban man, can the círculo be satisfied with devoting most of its educational energies to the development of rational and categorical thinking? By adopting directed learning for the círculos, Cuban educators must confront some of the paradoxical dilemmas inherent in this approach: Can children be both efficient and creative? Achievement-motivated and not anxiety-ridden? Highly disciplined and yet flexible? Are the Cubans prepared to accept docile conformity rather than spirited individual expression? If so, then total obeisance to the cause of directed learning should be the rule: the new Cuban man will be a drone in the service of the queen-bee state, rather than the creative and altruistic human being envisioned by Castro and Che. A Cuban critic of directed learning reminds the círculos: "If you go to a totally planned program you forget that there is such a thing as independence, which plays such an important role in the growth of character. There is also the need to make decisions at an appropriate time, an ability which does not fall as easily as manna from heaven." [49]

Much of the debate over the value of directed learning and its implications for Cuba is, in the end, irrelevant. For in my observations of the daily routine at the círculos I came away with the sharp realization that all the plans and programs discussed by the leadership rarely make their way down through the administrative funnel into the classroom. As with most school systems, I discovered that in Cuba, too, the rarefied atmosphere in which the critical issues are debated at the top is very different from the mundane environment found in the schools themselves. For Cuba, the problem of filtering the views of leadership down to the individual classroom is further frustrated by the quality of personnel. Most of those working directly with the children are so minimally trained that it is next to impossible to expect them to understand the implications of the philosophical positions held by the educators and psychologists in command. While headquarters carefully sticks pins into the educational map, detailing the required "attack" positions, those in the field—the asistentes in the círculos—frequently not only ignore the orders that come from the general staff, but do not even understand the nature of the battle.

Added to all this is the fact of everyday círculo life. As I have suggested, a simple accounting of the number of hours spent during a typical day on routine activities such as eating, bathing, diapering, changing clothes, napping, resting, and playing freely in the patio leaves few moments for even the most astute educator to concentrate on any of the ambitious plans for directed learning suggested by the leadership. I once asked an asistente whether she had any difficulty following the planeamientos prescribed for the círculos. "Oh, no!" she exclaimed. "No trouble at all. I can do everything they say to do in a few minutes!"

JARDINES INFANTILES

Without the historical precedent of any other socialist country, Cuba in 1965 started a second early-childhood school system, the jardines infantiles. While socialist systems rarely, if ever, allow themselves the luxury of competitive administrations, capitalist countries have of course had long experience with parallel school systems: public, private, and parochial. The jardín experiment, coexisting side-by-side with the national círculo system, developed into one of the most dramatic phenomena of the Cuban Revolution. Although ultimately suspended in 1971, it indicated that it was possible, even under socialism, to break away successfully from centralized control.

An Experiment

Initiated almost entirely by the efforts of Haydée Salas, a young woman who had taught biology before the Revolution, the jardines are modeled after Finnish garden day nurseries. Accompanying her husband on a diplomatic mission to Finland following the Revolution, Salas observed the rather free approach to nursery-school education in that country. Upon her return, and in reaction to what she observed in the círculos, she began a campaign to mold Cuban early-childhood education in the image of Finnish garden nurseries. Following discussions with psychologists and educators, she and her colleague Lela Sánchez formulated a plan for a day-care center on the Finnish model. Castro suggested that they start a pilot day-care center to test the project in 1964.

Salas and Sánchez enlisted the support of a number of Cuban organizations and individuals to aid in the establishment of a pilot unit; the planning department provided land, university students helped train personnel, and the Ministry of Public Health published a set of directives about childhood behavior for parents.[50] The central government offered little money or assistance. The two women worked voluntarily for the next four and a half years on the jardín project, while at the same time continuing their regular jobs; finally, they were assigned to full-time employment at the jardines.

While the jardines and the círculos used the same rhetoric concerning their long-range goals, they operated quite differently. The círculo system concentrates its attention on cleanliness, directed learning, and planned schedules, while the jardines relied on free play, exploration, and a relaxed, unplanned atmosphere.

According to Lela Sánchez, Cuba's chief motive for permitting the jardines to exist along with the círculos was the critical need to provide additional day-care centers at less cost and with fewer personnel.[51] Sánchez indicated, in an interview with Ruth Lewis, that Castro himself was concerned about the círculos, primarily because they required large staffs.[52] Círculo expansion was seriously blocked owing to the lack of a large enough work force: one adult asistente and two women workers were required for every eight to ten children. The jardines require three staff members per center, each of which can accommodate between thirty and fifty children.

The first jardín opened on January 1, 1965, in East Havana. It was followed by another in July of the same year in Miramar, Havana. A year later, the first jardín serving lunch was inaugurated, and by the end of 1966, 20 jardines were in operation. Rapid expansion followed. In 1967, there were 100 and by the end of 1968, 164. In September 1971, when the program was coming to an end, there were 178 in all, most of them in Havana; only a handful were in operation or under construction elsewhere. In all, the jardines were serving about 6000 children by the fall of 1971.

To help finance the project in the early experimental days, families were charged $7.50 per child per month. Later, various ministries and departments assisted with construction funds, architectural plans, employees' salaries, and food. The Ministry of Light Industry, for example, received a budget to provide the jardines with toys and furniture. Teachers earned $85.90 a month.

Depending upon the population of particular neighborhoods, some jardines had small or no waiting lists, while for others the lists were long. Children were accepted according to their mother's occupation, first preference being given to children whose mothers were engaged in agricultural work; next in line came the children of mothers who worked in factories; then came the children of women who did any other kind of work; and last, students' and housewives' children were admitted. Allegiance to the Revolution did not automatically open the doors, nor was revolutionary fidelity required.

Unlike the círculos, which offer day care to children forty-five days of age and older, jardines took only children from eighteen months on. At five years, children left the jardines for the elementary schools run by the Ministry of Education.

Although the jardines were inspired by the Finnish outdoor play schools, the Cubans transformed the Scandinavian system into a more sophisticated one. Without official sponsorship or a particular educational philosophy, the privately run Finnish play parks simply offer parents a relaxed place to send their preschool children. Cuban psychologists who appreciated many of the qualities of the Finnish system—such as outdoor play areas in the child's neighborhood, personal toys, caretakers who are called "aunts"—combined these features with modern theories of learning and development to create the peculiarly Cuban jardín.

Echoing círculo objectives, the jardines proclaimed their principles:

1. Achieve the best possible development of the child, thereby contributing to the creation of a new generation which will be physically, emotionally, and mentally better than previous generations.

2. Facilitate the integration of women into the work force and other social activities.

3. Integrate the child as an active presence into the urban structure, with corresponding effects upon society and the child.[53]

While the first two could well have been lifted verbatim from círculo literature, the third is a departure. Planned with the city child in mind, the jardín concentrated its efforts on his particular needs.

Physically, the jardines and círculos differ markedly. The círculo is a large, all-embracing structure, capable of housing a variety of functions and services. The jardín, on the other hand, opted for minimal housing, relying primarily on the outdoors. "Child-care centers are placed in green, open areas, in full view of the people—near the child's home." [54] Such an approach allowed the jardín leadership to boast that they constructed their facilities at minimum cost to the Revolution.

Literally a garden, the jardín consists of a spacious outdoor play area in which is set a small, all-purpose, prefabricated house large enough to accommodate cots, lunch tables, and chairs for about thirty children. A deliberately non-inhibiting childhood environment, the jardín is a playground which denies institutionalism. All administrative offices have been eliminated. The house itself is used only for meals, naps, and rainy-day activities.

The play area is eight or nine times greater than the building which is located at the back—in the part least visible to the child— so that from his very arrival he feels that the jardín is a playground. We have eliminated all those structures—director's and administrative offices—which the child regards as prohibited, since from his point of view they have nothing to do with his realm of knowledge. This is facilitated by the fact that everything for the jardín office can be stored on a closet shelf.

Also, the fence is small and camouflaged with vegetation. To the child, the fence should be nothing more than the line that sets off his play area, so he does not feel closed in and can see everything outside of the jardín's play area. In a way, this helps the child to begin to integrate himself into the everyday life of his environment (farm, town, or city)—a requirement for the child's complete development and socialization.[55]

Compared with the círculos, jardín enrollment is small. To avoid unnecessary conflict between school and home, the jardín simply does away with strict arrival-and-departure schedules. It is open only during working hours. Parents may leave or pick up their children at any time during the school day, Monday to Friday, 6 A.M. to 6 P.M. Haydée Salas explained the reason for the relaxed schedule: "If we said that the jardín starts at 8 A.M.—which many early-childhood programs do—this would mean that when the mother arrived at 8:15 with her child, the director and the mother would most likely argue about adherence to the 8 A.M. deadline. The child ends up right in the middle." [56] In one study surveying the attitudes of jardín parents, the vast majority indicated that of all the features of the jardines, the free schedule was the most desirable.[57]

Stressing the importance of parent-child relationships, the jardín believes that the family should be together during the dinner hour. Therefore, lunch and snacks are served, but not dinner; non-working mothers are required to take their children home for lunch. Unlike the círculo, the jardín neither bathes the child nor provides him with a uniform. Jardín day-care workers do not wear uniforms, either.

Jardines encourage the family to continue to assume many of the traditional home functions. Careful not to reduce the mother's feeling of commitment and responsibility to her child, the jardín seeks to integrate day care and family life; the jardín and the family should ideally interact symbiotically, so that the child's day-care experiences enrich his home life. The goal is for the child to feel that the same kind of behavior is expected in both home and school, thereby erasing any sense of conflict between the world and his family circle.

The jardines encourage mothers to stay with their children until the latter feel free enough to establish new relationships with the other children and the caretakers. (Recently, the círculos, too, have begun to suggest that mothers stay with children until they are ready to remain in the center for the full day.) In addition, the jardín promotes a sense of continuity between home and school by its location in the center of the neighborhood and by permitting the child to bring his own toys from home.

On my last visit to Cuba I asked Lela Sánchez how she reconciled the notion of the new Cuban man—who eschews all forms of private property—with the idea of bringing toys from home. Weren't they basically incompatible? Sánchez felt there was no contradiction: "In a communist society you must have your rights to your own pants and your own shirts. A communist society retains the idea of private property." Carrying this over to day care, she said, "When a child brings a toy to the jardín, he must lend it to the others. Social pressure causes him to do this. Slowly, he loses his egoism. You teach children the virtue of generosity in a way that will help them eliminate their normal feelings of egoism." [58]

Following a trend in early-childhood education in other countries, the jardines practice "inter-aged" education, in which children of all age groups join together in one class. D. E. M. Gardner, the British educator, reported on interaging in English nursery schools: "The younger and older children are encouraged to play together during part of the day, because the little ones learn much from the older and because their presence leads the older ones to help them." [59] "We believe in inter-aged mixing," echoed a jardín psychologist. "The little ones learn from the big ones and the big ones learn from the little ones—in play, in responsibility, they all learn." [60] As Sánchez noted, "We feel that from the age of one and a half to the age of four it is a very positive thing for children to be grouped together . . . it seems to us that at this early stage it is easier for a child to learn from other children than from an adult." Questioned as to whether children are influenced more by adults than by their peers, Sánchez indicated that despite the fact that children are instructed to listen to adults as guides to proper behavior, "in dealing, for example, with the problems of learning how to speak, the child learns more from someone closer to his own age" than from adults. Sánchez believes that children tend to imitate those who are closer in age and abilities, rather than the bigger and more distant adults. In addition, Sánchez suggests that children are equipped to assist one another in achieving adulthood together. "Ultimately, it is more stimulating for the child *not* to be separated from other children at a very young age, an age of great discovery." [61]

According to a jardín psychologist, "The jardín should be similar to a family with children of all ages. In a family there is a five-year-old, a seven-year-old and a three-year-old and although they do not have the same interests, they must learn to relate and discover their own interests through spontaneous play." [62]

Free Play

The jardín leadership believes that day care rests on two key principles: a belief in affective relationships between adults and children and the notion that play is a critical instrument which permits children to channel aggressive behavior into socially useful patterns. As one jardín psychologist explained, "Play is important because it meets the needs of all children. Inasmuch as every human being harbors within him the possibility of being aggressive, it is important to know how to handle the aggression." Cautioning against traditional approaches, the psychologist reasoned, "We can, if we want, attempt to domesticate the child. In the long run it will only lead to a negative person who is 'beaten' as a personality. Or we can help to channel aggressiveness into socially useful behavior—for this is a communist society. We don't want a sycophantic person who says 'Sí, señor,' or one who negatively says 'No' to everything without thinking. We want a person who can think independently and help us build a better society." [63]

There are two distinct approaches to play activities in day-care centers in Cuba. In the círculos, play is directed. To the jardín leadership, play is the child's translation of adult work. "For the preschool child, play is work. Play is his source of pleasure. Play means free play; play that isn't 'robbed' by overemphasis placed on adult areas of concentration—on cleanliness, eating, etc. These are adult concerns." [64]

The jardín leadership believes that its long-range approach is closer to Cuba's revolutionary aims than is that of the círculos. "We won't have the creative spirit in the new generation if the child is provided with too much structure and pre-established planned behavior. Within thirty years we won't have Cubans who will be capable of taking the initiative. Play, natural and free, is the key." [65]

The jardines have suggested in their own literature:

If we cannot be happy except when we see clean, obedient, inactive children, we cannot aspire to having a youth capable of sacrificing its personal comfort . . . to the exploration and investigation of ideals.

Our comforts . . . are the things that cause us to impede free play among children.

If we don't permit the child to play in the mud so that he can build his imaginary fort, we are teaching him that the care of his clothes is more important than the satisfaction of building or doing something new.[66]

Jardines favor plastic materials such as sand as playing tools because they have no defined structure or function; they allow children to project their feelings and ideas and to express their fantasies without acting out aggressively in antisocial ways. Clay, in particular, offers the child a chance both to construct and destroy an object without fear of reprisal. Every jardín boasts a sandbox. From a classical Freudian perspective, play with water and sand during the anal-oriented stage may act as a socially acceptable substitute for the child's desire to play with his own feces. It becomes an effective medium by which children may release some of their feelings of conflict over toilet training.

Free play offers children the chance to abide by their own particular developmental clock. While theory holds that all children progress more or less along similar lines, the specific needs of children during each stage vary; denying children the full range of freedom to explore their environment may slow their development. As Piaget has shown, a child does not learn mathematics by manipulating numbers, but rather by exploring its concepts in concrete form through play.[67]

Play is not only a source of pleasure, but one of the logistical supports of human growth. Through play, children learn to express themselves, work out problems, and master skills. Erik Erikson claims that the ultimate purpose of play is "to hallucinate ego mastery and yet also practice it in an intermediate reality between fantasy and actuality." [68]

In principle, if not always in practice, the círculos also appreciate the importance of play for child development. Yet, while the jardín focuses on free activities, the círculo uses play as a means to achieve certain defined objectives. *Simientes* encourages asistentes to understand the importance of play in the lives of children:

Asistentes who have not been instructed properly think that games are merely entertainment, the best way for children to spend a few pleasant hours. Children play because they enjoy it and are happy while playing. For an educator, play is more than a source of childish happiness, although this in itself is a lot. For the asistente who knows her job, play is a valuable means of educating the child. It is the most efficient instrument for carrying out the educational mission, taking advantage of the great interest of the children in games to make them proficient in many skills and to develop a large number of abilities. For example, when children play hide and seek they are developing their attention and memory skills. First, they concentrate on verifying which companions are still there (the attentive process), then they try to remember who has hidden (memory). It is obvious that the children are unaware of all of this and play for the sake of playing; but the educator knows why and is clearly aware of the educational process in motion. As a result she directs the activity with enthusiasm and efficiency. If she is unaware of the educational value in these games and reduces them to a simple diversion, it is possible that she will always remain passive and will limit herself to watching the behavior of the little ones.[69]

While both jardín and círculo day-care workers are urged to be loving and kind to children, they see their roles from different philosophical perspectives. Encouraged to intervene in the learning and socialization processes of child development, círculo asistentes structure the environment according to prescribed stages. The jardín worker is trained to interfere as little as possible. She may suggest to a child who has gone beyond the bounds of acceptable behavior that he be seated in a chair away from the rest of the group. "If the teacher is too authoritarian the child will not like her," Sánchez stated. "The teacher's ideas will be rejected by the child." [70]

In principle, the caretaker in the jardín is a signpost to indicate the limits of socially undesirable behavior, while not inhibiting the child's natural spontaneity. Theoretically, the limited number of jardín asistentes also serves to provide children with just a few important objects of affection and trust; each one then takes on a real significance. Gerwitz warned that each caretaker at a day-care center gives the child a different set of stimuli which may provide incompatible sets of demands and rewards, confusing the child's ability to respond consistently.[71] Too many caretakers may overtax the child's ability to adapt and ultimately rob the environment of the consistency required for healthy development.

Sánchez noted: "The jardín is a place where the teacher feels confident that the children can play as hard as they want, but it is also a place where they will be safe." [72]

As Ruth Lewis observed, "There is much toughening of the children in free play. There is an active process of socialization rather than passive." In contrast to children in the círculos who are "told what to do with their hands and bodies, told not to run, stand, hit, etc., in the jardín they learn appropriate behavior by experiencing the need for it." Yet Lewis objected to the lack of experiences in sharing, as well as to inadequate adult guidance and the amorphous sense of discipline. "The jardín is too disorganized and free floating. There is too much fighting, pushing, pulling, venting of aggressions—especially on the smaller, younger, more passive ones, and not enough conscious effort by the teachers to socialize the children." [73]

Critics of the jardines claim that older children do not receive enough stimulation; those who have passed the stage of working out their difficulties in achieving socialization through play should be ready to accept more intellectually taxing activities. And younger children, who almost always require more protection in a narrower circle of play, may find themselves lost in the wide latitude offered by the jardín.

Nonetheless, there is no evidence one way or another which allows educators to accept the notion that laissez-faire upbringing will guarantee the kind of Cuban citizen idealized by the new Cuban man. Psychologists are coming to the conclusion that children not only need limits to their behavior, but desire it from adults not only in subtle but often in rather obvious ways. Thus perhaps the jardín's reliance on non-directed learning to achieve revolutionary goals could not in fact have helped produce Castro's dream of the future man. In their overreaction to the highly organized círculo school, jardín psychologists may have gone too far.

So much remains unknown about developing children that it is almost impossible to predict what early-childhood conditions will produce an expected set of qualities. Yet choices must be made, and schools usually employ that system which best reflects a society's idea of how children ought to behave and the goals that they should aim for as adults. If day care anywhere adopts the directed-learning approach, it must, to succeed, be moderated by a set of human principles which allows for normal differences between children, and which considers them as unique bodies and minds and not as objects to be manipulated in the cause of higher grades and better test scores. Alternatively, if centers operate in a laissez-faire atmosphere, then they must take steps to mitigate chaos by structuring some activities, offering adult leadership, and providing acceptable guidelines for normal childhood behavior. The jardines in Cuba had a vision which one hopes will find its way ultimately into day-care philosophy.

The men of tomorrow are the children we are forming today. A child who remains clean all of the time, who is not permitted contact with nature, who fears everything which is not within the limits of an excessively organized, stable, and secure life, will not be a man capable of facing new and different situations, nor of giving up his security and comforts in order to undertake the struggles necessary for his freedom or that of other peoples and the control and transformation of nature.[74]

IV ★ NUTRITION AND HEALTH CARE

One might expect a report on nutrition and health care of Cuban young children to be found most readily in a work on current pediatric practice, or in a volume on public health. Such matters as the care and feeding of young children might seem out of place in a book devoted to the young child and his school environment. But in Cuba, health care is linked with education. Nutritious and adequate food, together with proper hygienic and health standards, are central to Cuban schools. New research in the United States and elsewhere endorses this conception.[1] Studies indicate that nutrition during early childhood affects both physical growth and mental functioning. For the poor, failure at school may result not only from a lack of some significant fundamental learning experiences at home, but also from nutritional and physiological poverty. In the past, educators have focused all their attention on the mind of the child, ignoring his biology. Ira J. Gordon, director of the Institute for Development of Human Resources at the University of Florida, expressed the need to integrate health care with early-childhood education:

The delivery of medical services and the delivery of educational services will most likely come closer and closer together as we recognize the value of the old Latin slogan, *Mens sana in corpore sano*—a sound mind in a sound body. To assign the mind to school and the body some place else makes little sense.[2]

The growing worldwide crisis of the poor—not only in economically underdeveloped nations but in many areas of the United States—prompted educators to prescribe massive doses of early "compensatory" educational experiences in what was seen as a dramatic attack on breaking the cycle of "cultural deprivation" and, it was hoped, making school rewarding for poor children. Enriched educational programs alone, however, proved inadequate, for they often failed to break the pattern of school failure, a norm among poor children for years. Reports from U.S. Head Start programs indicated that those poor children who ostensibly were offered enriched curricula at an early age in the long run often responded no better than those who entered school without the benefit of these "culturally and cognitively enriched" programs. [3] Even after the introduction of significant early learning experiences, these children did not or could not respond effectively. In many circles, pessimism prevailed.

It was believed that poor children were locked into an endless failure cycle, no matter what educators did to try to break the pattern. They were poor; they struggled at school; they failed. After leaving school, they again failed; the demands of the technologically dominated economy awaiting them were too great to meet. Ultimately, they raised children in the same environment in which they were trapped. Herbert G. Birch and Joan Dye Gussow report that "In the newly emerging countries it has been recognized that educational failure is part of a cycle of poverty, social ineffectiveness, and ignorance that is repetitive unless the links which bind its component parts are broken." [4] For a graphic rendering of this interrelationship, see Figure 2. [5]

In order to stop this cycle of failure, Cuba has instituted a program that cares for the child's physical as well as educational needs. The child is viewed as a whole human being with each part deserving its rightful attention. Cuban day care developed a dramatically effective program to attend to the child's biological needs first; "cognitive and cultural" requirements often take second place. If intellectual development is based exclusively on the cognitive and verbal environment of children, it was argued, one loses sight of the physical, cultural, and social forces that shape intelligence and speech. One must recognize the physiological functions of children and consequently the necessity of a positive medical and nutritional environment to facilitate intellectual achievement.

From the Cuban viewpoint, traditional nursery-school care, offering only peer-group socialization under the guidance of professional educators, is not enough. Group play, development of motor activies, cognitive development, and other educational components of early-childhood education are, of course, understood to be fundamental nursery-

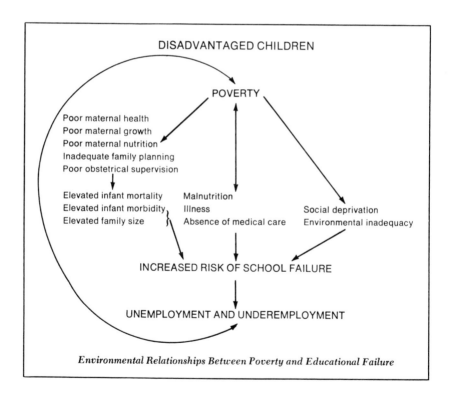

Environmental Relationships Between Poverty and Educational Failure

school activities. However, perhaps most importantly, schools also take on roles traditionally left to the home. "Without a healthy mental and corporal base one cannot speak of correct integral education," Clementina Serra pointed out. [6] Good health care then becomes an inalienable right of children.

According to the círculo leadership there are two facets of early-childhood education. One is quantitative, growth; the other, qualitative, development. Growth, in the Cuban vocabulary, means the "increased mass due to cellular multiplication." Development "implies the acquisition of new functions." [7] Diet, health, and cleanliness form the quantitative educational trinity, while the qualitative concerns the development of capacities and skills, and the formation of attitudes and habits. In addition to a proper emotional environment offering understanding and satisfying the child's basic needs, the círculos outline these basic rules for assuring that both the qualitative and quantitative aspect of growth and development receive their due:

- Hygienic and spacious schools, full of air and sunshine.
- A balanced diet which meets the nutritional requirements of each age level.
- Preventive medicine, coupled with routine observations of childhood growth and development.[8]

HYGIENE

Personal hygiene is a ubiquitous feature of the early-childhood program. "Cleanliness is the key word" [9] in the círculos. An observer unprepared for the emphasis placed on cleanliness in the nursery schools would immediately draw the conclusion that this concern was carried to the point of fetishism.

When the children arrive in the morning their street clothes are removed and they are dressed in communally shared uniforms, [10] which are washed daily at the day-care center itself. All the children's clothing and any other items used in the círculo are washed by hand; washing machines are in short supply.

Each child is bathed every day. All adults must put on a sterilized smock on entering an infant room. Those who feed babies must wear face masks. Each infant room usually adjoins a separate changing and bathing area. While some children are being bathed, the others are sometimes left unattended. Thus, although the círculo leadership claims that the ratio of adult personnel to children is one to ten, there are often times when the ratio is much higher.

When the círculo leadership outlines its principal objectives in what it calls "corporal and psychic health," invariably at the top of the list stands "clean and spacious environments." Proper diet, preventive medical care, and emotional stability usually follow in that order.

Consuelo Miranda notes:

Our children must live in very open spaces because our climate demands it. Naturally, children get dirtier in open spaces than they do indoors. And if they get dirty more often, we must wash them more often. Very often, we let the children play on the floor where it is cooler and where they can move around more freely. Naturally, we have to be sure that floors are kept clean. Also, the child who has been playing in the patio all morning—running, jumping, leaping—must be bathed because he is covered with sweat. We can't let a child eat or nap like that. We must bathe him to let him sit at the table. If he runs again in the afternoon, we must bathe him again. We can't allow him to be sweaty because he will suffer eruptions on the skin, bad odor, etc.[11]

The high status of bathing in the círculo routine is indicated by the exhaustive detail of an article by the Department of Health of the Círculos Infantíles in *Simientes*.

The order in which the body is washed is always the same: first the face and hair and then the rest of the body. The hair need not be washed every day. Starting with the small tots, it's necessary to do so twice a week (especially in the case of girls), except on very hot days or when, due to other circumstances, the need might arise for more frequent hair washings. As the child grows older, we encourage him to do things by himself in the bath; we teach him to dry his toes well, to put on his clothes, his socks, his shoes (even though he isn't able to manage the laces) and so on.

Not satisfied with prescribing the bath ritual in its precise order, the Department of Health then recommends proper use of the articles accompanying the bath. For example:

1. Each child must have his individual towel; there is no reason to justify drying more than one child with the same towel.

2. Towels should be washed and boiled every day. If this is not possible, they should be marked, well isolated one from another and put out to dry thoroughly in the sun before they are used again. In any case, they should never be used more than twice.

3. If there are enough washcloths to go around, these should be used. As soon as bath time is over, they should be boiled for use on the following day. If it is not possible to follow these measures because there are not enough washcloths, children should be bathed without them, since we cannot allow more than one child to be bathed with the same washcloth.

4. Face towels used by the children to dry their hands and faces when they have their meals or "go to the bathroom," etc., must also be for individual use. The towels should be marked so that each child uses his own, or better still, they can be put into a laundry bag and a clean one used the next time.[12]

In cleanliness, too, the jardines departed vigorously from the círculos. The jardines thought the proper place to practice hygiene was in the home; day care should allow children to get as dirty as they wish. According to Lela Sánchez.

"Bathing is a very intimate thing for the child. It should not be the task of anyone but the mother. Mothers have always done it, whether they are working mothers or not." Sánchez noted, "At the mother's hands the child will not receive machine-like treatment. If the mother is responsible for bathing her child, she cannot easily lose affection or closeness with the child. Our hopes for the child's health development are founded on the relationship he has with his parents." She added, "While we develop those hygienic habits that are necessary, we let the child play freely without allowing clean hands and clean clothes to limit him in any way. We in no way sacrifice the child's freedom to play in order to keep him clean, pretty, and sweet smelling." [13]

Often, the emphasis on cleanliness and order is tied to socialist goals. In one "pedagogical orientation" for círculo asistentes, it was suggested that in order to build "a better understanding of socialist norms and the care of socialist property," asistentes should "unite the children of the various groups and tell them to unify their efforts in cleaning up the dead leaves." To promote a "conscious attitude" among the children, the círculo staff is directed to have them care for toys, clothing, and other materials in the classroom. [14]

In the final analysis, one can attribute the Cuban concentration on cleanliness to two principal factors: culture and climate. Cubans have traditionally shown an overriding concern with personal hygiene and environmental cleanliness. Even before the Revolution, visitors were struck by the seemingly endless care the people took with their surroundings. This cultural phenomenon—encouraged by the tropical climate which requires that one keep one's surroundings and person cool in the heat of the powerful sun—persists today in the círculos and in the everyday life of the people. Bathing and powdering not only are practices which Cubans follow with their children; they are patterns of everyday life for most of the population. Following the U.S. blockade, when soaps and deodorants were hard to come by, the Cubans created many substitutes to satisfy their personal needs. It is not unusual to find that Cubans have transmitted their sensitivity to cleanliness and personal hygiene to their children, particularly since most Cubans believe that children are more susceptible than adults to diseases caused by unhygienic conditions.

Added to this is the fact that the círculos were entrusted with the duty to serve children of the urban and rural poor who, in many cases, were not equipped to handle the problems of cleanliness. Since many homes in the countryside, as well as in the city, lacked adequate toilet and bathing facilities, it was felt that the schools had an obligation to these families to care for the cleanliness of their children.

In addition, and despite the fact that Cuban values support strict personal hygiene, there are families that do not practice the kind of physical cleanliness thought adequate. The círculos, then, assumed the responsibility for encouraging what they felt to be proper hygienic habits among all the children in their charge, so that those children whose families do not practice proper cleanliness might receive appropriate instruction at school.

The círculo planeamiento suggests that habits of cleanliness and order be introduced during the child's first week at school. The teacher is given these recommendations: "Comment on how we are impressed by the children who always arrive on time, whose shoes are clean, and who take good care of their uniforms. Tell how we feel when we see the room is clean and neat." [15]

Toilet training, as a part of hygiene, is treated rather matter-of-factly. Certain standard patterns of behavior are expected from the child at a particular stage in his development and, according to Garrity, children in the círculos accept the norms and behave accordingly. [16] Asked about the círculo's perspective on toilet training, Miranda replied: "We wait until the normal age at which control is possible and then we begin to stimulate the child to take on the responsibility by frequently inviting him to the potty-chair, asking him whether he wants to move his bowels or urinate. Then we show our delight when the child begins to advise us of his necessities." [17] Toilet training begins after the children have left the lactante-baby room, or at about one year old. The círculos claim that they do not coerce children to become toilet trained, but in practice it appears that Cubans demand rather strict conformity.

The psychological repercussions of cleanliness in the círculos may not be fully appreciated by Cuba's educational leadership. Such strict attention to keeping children clean may have damaging effects on them; it is not unlikely that forcing children to stay clean despite their other activities may induce feelings of guilt and anxiety. Erikson warns that outer controls established by authorities may not be compatible with the child's inner ability to accept them. [18] If Erikson is correct, the círculos' insistence on cleanliness may trigger a child's fears and anxieties concerning his physical being and growth. Day care unquestionably has a creative role to play in the formation of hygienic habits, but it is not altogether clear whether the Cuban círculo's single-mindedness about cleanliness is satisfied with good habits, or whether it actually prefers children who are abnormally concerned with keeping clean. While day care has an obligation to keep children safe from disease by offering an environment that is at once safe and healthy, preschool education cannot be effective if children spend so much time in the bath at the expense of the playground.

NUTRITION

The relationship between poor diet and poor intellectual growth has yet to be conclusively demonstrated, yet recent investigations indicate that improper nutrition may lead to serious intellectual shortcomings in children. Studies, mostly with animals, show that malnutrition early in life can cause permanent chemical changes in the brain. Research has revealed that the number of brain cells in rats, as well as in humans, can be reduced if they are fed insufficient diets at early ages. Similarly, other brain and bodily functions can be seriously impaired by poor nutrition during infancy. The precise relationship between these chemical changes and intellectual function is not yet fully understood. Nevertheless, investigations with children in Latin America, Asia, and Africa tend to show that malnutrition may be a principal cause of certain learning disabilities. More data will be needed to demonstrate whether or not improper diet leads to poor classroom performance.[19] However, it has long been observed that lack of proper nutrients decreases a child's productivity. Missing essential vitamins, minerals, and proteins, the body protects itself by avoiding the expenditure of energy; in the end, the nutrient-deficient child becomes apathetic and lethargic. Scientific research is not necessary to conclude that children who are hungry or who are given nutritionally deficient diets do not come to school as prepared for intellectual stimulation as do their classmates who have had a decent meal.

Philosophically, Cuban educators believe that proper diet promotes effective learning at school and so, in practice, they have made the delivery of good nutrition a central responsibility of the círculos. The Cubans feel, as do other educators, that schools must offer more than enriched educational programs at earlier and earlier ages; they must provide good nutrition as well.

Considered the "élite," the *raison d'être* of the Revolution, Cuban children receive greater supplies of milk, chicken, meat, fruits, and vegetables than do their parents. While the rationing system severely limits supplies to adults, rationing does not really affect preschoolers, who receive the first shipments of foods that are available.

The círculos introduced some foods with which many Cubans were not familiar. In many communities before the Revolution, for example, milk was disliked; medical workers and círculo personnel discovered children suffering from diseased mouths and badly decayed teeth. In Gran Tierra, the people had not eaten fish before the círculo arrived. In other parts of the country, the círculos were the first to introduce meat, eggs, and other foods. In some backwoods areas, rice, beans, and root vegetables were the basic diet before the Revolution.

Recognizing that the backgrounds and family customs of school chefs and kitchen personnel may not have included balanced, healthy diets, the círculos do not permit free choice in menu planning in local schools. In order to guarantee food standards, the National Administration of Nutrition and Diet prepared a diet manual,[20] approved by the Ministry of Public Health pediatric office. Used in círculos throughout Cuba, the manual suggests different menus for all meals, including snacks; recipes offer approved quantities for different age levels. They also include food substitutes in cases where "temporary difficulty," shortages, or special conditions within a region do not permit an individual círculo to follow the suggested menu. Table 11 shows the number of calories needed for healthy development according to U.S. sources, and Table 12 indicates the prescribed caloric intake for children in

Cuban day-care centers. Círculo children have a more than ample caloric intake in terms of U.S. health standards.[21]

The ten menus in the diet manual offer adequate proteins, fats, carbohydrates, vitamins, and minerals. Milk, cheese, eggs, fruits, poultry, fish, meat, cereals, butter, and vegetables are all represented in the daily menus. Menu 1, as shown in Table 13, gives the diet for children fourteen months to six years of age. Of course, the dishes vary with each meal; the other nine suggested plans are given in Table 14.

Table 11: Recommended U.S. Daily Calorie Standard

Age	Calories
1–2 months	480
2–6 months	770
6 months–1 year	900
1–2 years	1100
2–3 years	1250
3–4 years	1400
4–6 years	1600

SOURCE: Food and Nutrition Board, National Academy of Sciences–National Research Council, "Recommended Daily Dietary Allowances," rev. ed., mimeographed (Washington, D.C., 1968).

Because of centralized educational planning and organization, similar menus are offered in rural areas and at schools in Havana and other cities. As shown in Table 15, the diet manual also guides schools in scheduling the ten daily menus throughout the month.

For lactantes, specific food requirements are also spelled out; these are organized by age into roughly three-month segments: forty-five days to three months, three months to six months, six to nine months, and nine to fourteen months. Formulas are prepared according to strict guidelines covering ingredients and equipment. Rules for introducing solid foods are also given.[22] Between six and nine months, meat is served in homogenized form or *en conserva*

Table 12: Daily Calories Offered in Círculo Diets

Age	Calories
1–3 months	730
4–9 months	995
10–12 months	1125
1–3 years	1300
3–6 years	1700

SOURCE: Ministerio de Salud Pública, *Manual de dietética para círculos infantiles,* mimeographed (Havana, 1963), p. 5.

Table 13: Círculo Diet Manual (Menu 1)
(14 months to 6 years)

Meal	Time	Food	Serving
Break-fast	7:30 A.M.	cereal	¼–½ cup
		toast	½–1 piece
		butter	½–1 pat
		milk	4 ounces
		orange juice or	
		tomato juice	4 ounces
Merienda (snack)			
Lunch	11:00 A.M.	vegetable soup	¼–½ cup
		roast chicken	¼ chicken
		guava jelly	¼–½ cup
		milk	4 ounces
Dinner	5:00 P.M.	pumpkin and malanga purée	2–5 spoonfuls
		picadillo de carne (beef hash)	1–3 ounces
		toast	½–1 piece
		banana	1–2
		milk	4 ounces

SOURCE: Ministerio de Salud Pública, Manual de dietética para círculos infantiles, mimeographed (Havana, 1963), p. 23.

Table 14: Círculo Diet Manual (Menus 2–10)
(14 months to 6 years)

Menu Number	Meal	Menu
2	lunch	boiled eggs, rice, bean purée
	dinner	soup, potato purée, carrot mix
3	lunch	spaghetti with meat, beets
	dinner	bean purée, chopped ham, salad
4	lunch	liver, plantains, string bean salad
	dinner	malanga soup, boiled eggs, vegetables
5	lunch	black bean purée, scrambled eggs, plantains
	dinner	fish soup, malanga purée
6	lunch	beet salad, corn mix, meat, and squash
	dinner	meat-base soup, baked chicken with vegetables
7	lunch	black bean purée, white rice, boiled eggs
	dinner	cream soup, beef stew
8	lunch	plantain soup, ground ham, vegetables
	dinner	*chícharo* purée, string beans and carrots, boiled steak
9	lunch	baked fish, vegetable soup
	dinner	root vegetable purée, baked beef with vegetables
10	lunch	baked bean purée, chopped meat, white rice
	dinner	green vegetable soup, fried plantains, boiled eggs

SOURCE: Ministerio de Salud Pública, *Manual de dietética para círculos infantiles,* mimeographed (Havana, 1963), pp. 27–34.

(bottled). After the first week fresh ground meat is served. *Vísceras* (liver, kidneys, etc.) and fish are later included in the diet. A menu is then drawn up for each day; Table 16 shows the different courses offered.

Eating time is pleasant and perhaps the greatest inter-active period of the círculo routine. As Garrity indicates, "Eating seemed to be one of the few times for caretakers, asistentes, and children to talk and look individually at one another." [23] Asistentes usually treat children warmly and personally at meals. Cuban children do not often refuse the food offered them.

Peggy Schirmer, on a visit to the Cárdenas school, witnessed children leaving a free-play situation to take juice from trays set out by asistentes, but this appears to be the

---

Table 15: Guide to Preparation of Círculo Daily Menus

		Menu Numbers			
Mon-day	Tues-day	Wednes-day	Thurs-day	Friday	Satur-day
1	2	3	4	5	6
7	8	9	10	1	2
3	4	5	6	7	8
9	10	1	2	3	4

SOURCE: Ministerio de Salud Pública, *Manual de dietética para círculos infantiles*, mimeographed (Havana, 1963), p. 25.

exception rather than the rule.[24] Most often, asistentes distribute food individually to each child. The atmosphere at meals is relaxed, giving, and individualized. At one círculo, as.a sleeping child awoke in his crib in a lactante unit at the Raúl Pérez school, an asistente picked him up, talked to him, changed his diaper, fed him, and placed him in one of the corrals. With three asistentes in the room, one was free

Table 16: Menu for Lactantes Following the Introduction of Meat	
Course	Choice of
1	soup cereal vegetables
2	meat (ground or chopped) egg (fried or boiled)
3	fruit (fresh, compote)

SOURCE: Ministerio de Salud Pública, *Manual de dietética para círculos infantiles,* mimeographed (Havana, 1963), p. 14.

to pick up waking children or "fuss" with the others. The asistentes held the small children, fed them from bottles, and gave them solid food. At another center, twenty-eight children between the ages of one and a half and two and a half sat at four tables. An asistente sat at each table helping children with their food while chatting with asistentes at the other tables. The women moved freely among the children, helping those who needed it. At one table, where the trays had already been removed and the asistente left to do other chores, the children started pounding their fists, shouting, "¡Agua!" At last, when the water arrived, the revolution at that table slowly subsided. As previously noted, such unruly behavior is quite rare; but since mealtime is the most relaxed period, it is not surprising that children find that they are freer to express themselves than during other times of the day.

Guidelines for asistentes caring for the eighteen-month to two-and-a-half-year-olds suggest that children should be kept away from the tables if meals are delayed. Once seated, children should be placed at the tables according to their ability to use a spoon: those who know how to eat well should be seated at one table, away from the others. Asistentes are instructed to give special attention to those who have not learned to eat by themselves, and they are encouraged to teach the children proper table habits, so that after eight weeks they can feed themselves. A rather rigid set of criteria decrees that during meals asistentes should see to the following:

That the children use the spoon properly.
That they do not mix different foods together.
That they eat everything that is served.
That they drink their milk.
That their faces and hands are clean.
That their noses are kept clean if they have colds.

These strict instructions are followed by a note which cautions asistentes to handle meals "without shouting or disturbing the children so that they may eat in peace." [25]

Food—and all things associated with eating—gives Cubans a very special kind of pleasure. Cooking, preparing meals, and fussing with recipes and holiday dishes have long been a "national sport." Today, rationing has further accented the focus on food. In some way, food and the pleasure it offers defines the Cuban. Eating the right food, prepared in the correct fashion, makes a Cuban feel satisfied as a human being. I was often startled to find that many Cubans would rather not buy fish, even when it was plentiful and other foods scarce; fish is not very much appreciated, and they would rather prepare a meal with a meager few ounces of strictly rationed beef.

MEDICAL CARE

Medical care is another key ingredient of the health program. The national public health agency, the Ministry of Public Health, joins with the círculos to deliver modern medical attention and is responsible for medical supervision at each círculo. In addition to offering preventive care for children and all personnel, MINSAP controls the hygienic environment and provides health-care guidelines for parents.

Prior to the child's admission to the círculo, parents must show the doctor the record of the child's checkups from the local polyclinic, hospital, or Mutualist Integrated Clinic. Without these records, the doctor is obliged to refuse to enroll the child. Upon admission to a círculo each child receives a number of tests and inoculations, including a complete clinical examination, tuberculosis, diphtheria, and hemoglobin tests, and a battery of vaccinations. The doctor maintains the child's complete clinical history once he is enrolled in the círculo. The physician assigned to the círculo treats infectious diseases and supervises the children's health care. He watches over the growth and development of each child, periodically checking his height, weight, cranial circumference, teething, and psychomotor development. The schools require three check-ups in the first semester, two in the second, and two annual check-ups thereafter. TB tests are prescribed every six months for children under three, annually thereafter. A parasitological examination of fecal material is taken every six months, and blood tests are administered whenever necessary. Children receive vaccinations against polio, TB, tetanus, diphtheria, and other diseases.[26]

Together with the asistentes and school psychologist, the physician is expected to coordinate psychosocial-pedagogical development programs (nutritional and eliminatory habits, language, and adaptive and social conduct). Moreover, these doctors—in cooperation with dietitians—prescribe and supervise the preparation of formulas and diets. The physicians also run educational programs for parents and school personnel. Together with the director, psychologist, and nurse or teacher, each trimester the doctor is expected to educate parents about the health of their children in lectures and through films and other audiovisual material. Educational programs for school personnel are given to enlighten them on such topics as hygiene and epidemiology.

The círculo also provides complete dental care for all children, direct responsibility for which rests with the polyclinic, hospital or dental clinic in the community. Each child over the age of three is given a complete dental examination and all necessary treatment. Dentists are expected to give sodium fluoride to children at ages three and five, take X-rays, treat oral infections, clean teeth (every twelve months), repair decayed teeth, treat teeth damaged by accidents, treat gums, and perform orthodonture. Like the doctors, dentists are also responsible for educational programs for parents and personnel, as well as for children.

V ★ THE FAMILY AND THE COMMUNITY

The Revolution changed many things. It brought literacy to the campesino in the remotest part of the island, tractors and roads to backwater villages, and military fatigues on the broad avenues of Havana. Maurice Zeitlin has observed: "Scarcely an aspect of the pre-revolutionary social structure in Cuba has remained intact, primarily because of the expropriation of the former owning classes, the virtual elimination of private property in the system of production and distribution, and the establishment of a centrally planned, publicly owned economy." [1]

One would expect such dramatic events to have precipitated a momentous alteration in the dynamics of family life. On the contrary, in Cuba the family persists. Thus far, the massive, rapid collectivization of the productive forces of the economy has not dealt a heavy blow to the intimate relationships between parents and children. The revolutionary leadership has not seen the necessity for collectivizing the family along with the economy, despite the fact that classical Marxism predicted not only the withering away of the state under socialism but the destruction of the nuclear family.

Friedrich Engels predicted that after the "impending effacement of capitalist production," men and women would enter into relationships in which the men will not have reason "to purchase a woman's surrender either with money or with any other means of social power" and the women in this new society will never be forced to "surrender to any man out of any consideration other than that of real love" and will not worry about "giving themselves to their beloved for fear of the economic consequences." Engels foresaw the demise of traditional marriage between socialist men and women. "Once such people appear, they will not care a rap about what we today think they should do. They will establish their own practice and their own public opinion, comfortable therewith, on the practice of each individual—and that's the end of it." [2]

If the economic and political structure of the community has been collectivized, what need is there for the anomalously bourgeois family? The traditional family supports a world view that is opposed to the development of the new socialist person. Antithetical to the collective model, the bourgeois unit offers autocratic parental rule, demand for private property in the home, exclusivity, and above all, individualism. Children "belong" to their parents as an automobile is owned by its driver.

In pre-revolutionary Cuba the family formed the fundamental institution. According to a 1935 Foreign Policy Association report of its Commission on Cuban Affairs, "None of the other forms of social organization is comparable to the strength of the Cuban family." It noted that the family in Cuba "displays greater solidarity and strength, and plays a much more important role in the total social organization, than in the commercialized cultures with which Cuban society is compared." [3]

Following the lead of other socialist nations, Cuba supported the conventional family, and, like the Soviet Union, took the position that child rearing should not only strengthen the family but at the same time call attention to the child's social role and responsibilities both within and outside the family unit. In the USSR, initial attempts to supersede the pre-revolutionary family with collective child-rearing experiments failed. The Soviets finally persuaded themselves that the traditional family should continue to be supported; after fifty years of economic and political collectivization, the Soviet family is as strong as ever. A. S. Makarenko advised in *The Collective Family*, the child-rearing guide used widely by parents in the Soviet Union: "If you wish to give birth to a citizen and do without parental love, then be so kind as to warn society that you wish to play such an underhanded trick. People brought up without parental love are often deformed people." [4] First published in 1937, *The Collective Family* has gone through a number of editions and has been read by great numbers of parents in the Soviet Union as well as in other socialist countries.

Makarenko dismissed wide-scale institutional upbringing for most Soviet children, and believed that the best child-rearing agency was the family.[5] Although he had great success with institutionalized problem children, he was opposed to large-scale efforts to rear children in boarding schools.

The Cubans encourage strong family relationships linked to day care. One Cuban day-care leader notes, "The círculos do not wish to sever child-parent relationships. On the contrary, we wish to stimulate them. We are slow to take children for boarding because we do not think it healthy that a child separate himself from the family in a permanent way. We only take them into boarding schools when we find no other solution." [6]

Even though day-care centers are open for children as young as forty-five days old, they do not encourage sleeping in. Boarding schools are available for children in the sixth grade and beyond, but only during high school do these becados become a significant feature of the educational program. The home is considered the place where young children learn to develop the Eriksonian sense of trust provided by loving, devoted parent figures.

But children reared in the traditional home environment often do not fare well either. That loving, kind people are good for children is not to be questioned; that all mothers and fathers are loving and kind to their own children is not always true. Even those parents who claim that they know what is best for their children may be those who know least. Our prejudices in favor of the mother caring for her child must succumb to the weight of evidence which tells us that it is not the only way. Perhaps it may not even be the best way to raise creative, healthy, trusting, intelligent offspring.

As Miranda lamented in an interview

In some cases the home is totally negative. A home is good for the child when it is a real home, when there is love, understanding, when the home can provide for the child's needs. When there is discord in the home, when there are misunderstandings between members of the household, when there are unhygienic conditions, when the child lacks attention, when there is nothing positive for him there—absolutely nothing—then it is good to take the child and place him into boarding school.

On the other hand, Miranda clearly indicated that

nothing can substitute for the ideal home, a home with extraordinary understanding between mother and father, a tranquil home where the child has everything he needs—sun, play, food. But the problem with these ideal homes is that there are very few of them in the world. In all worlds—even in the capitalist world.[7]

In defense of the círculos, Miranda argued that they do not exhibit any of the negative features of "institutionalism." She believes that institutionalism develops from the notion of charity and welfare. Since Cuban early-childhood programs are based not on need but on a national effort to encourage all children to attend, she finds that círculos do not produce any of the emotional handicaps commonly associated with institutional care.[8]

Ira J. Gordon points out that

not only in disadvantaged but also in so-called advantaged families in the United States, the parent as potent modeler is not necessarily present or functional. That is, parents may lack the time, skill, or inclination to establish warm emotional relationships with their children, and to provide them with their standards of behavior.[9]

The conventional wisdom believes that the natural mother is the best, and in fact the only, figure capable of offering her child the kind of trust that Erikson says is required for healthy and natural development. Obviously the neglected, the orphaned, the abandoned child, thrown into a public institution, often fails to grow into a warm, trusting, loving human being. He understands quite early that life offers no refuge and that trust is hollow. The institutionalized child grows up a pale, suffering shell of person.

Whether at home or at school, the Cubans believe that they can systematically encourage the growth and development of the child's capacities and abilities in order to foster certain attitudes in accordance with the national philosophy, to establish socially acceptable habits, and to initiate him, at a very early age, as to the value of the collective experience as opposed to the individual one. These educational processes, according to the Cubans, can take place so long as the home and school together recognize the way in which children grow and develop. "Education begins with life itself," Miranda proclaimed, "and it is the responsibility of the society to establish the institutions and the means which are adequate for its effective realization." [10]

Cuban psychologists and educators also stress the need for supportive, loving, familiar relationships throughout the child's life: "The first social learning of the child takes place in the home, and the first experiences with his family, especially with his mother, are decisive in the determination of the child's attitude toward others," reported Cuban psychologists Léon and Martínez. "The child is totally helpless, depending on the mother for the fulfillment of his vital needs. This situation of extreme dependence creates the conditions that explain the tremendous molding force that the mother's conduct has on the development of the child's personality." [11]

The Cubans, believing that stable, informed families offer one of the best routes toward healthy, productive children, have made an intense effort to strengthen and educate the family. Miranda notes:

There is a burgeoning interest on the part of the parents in knowing how their child grows and develops: which are the favorable factors, what situations may have harmful results, and what they as parents can do to contribute to the better fulfillment of these processes. There is an ever-increasing public demand for books, magazines, and documentaries dealing with the education of children from the cradle on, and consequently, it has become necessary to intensify and extend the means of publication and distribution so as to supply parents with necessary information on a massive scale.[12]

In 1966, Castro himself, at the closing session of a national meeting of school monitors, * encouraged parents to meet their responsibilities toward their children:

The greatest offense that can be committed against a human being and against society, the gravest offense that a father or a mother can commit, is to permit his child not to attend school. It will not be the law, it will not be the coercive force of the state, but, rather, social conscience that imposes on each citizen the idea that he cannot commit the crime of creating an ignoramus or of bringing an ignoramus into the world.[13]

* Monitors are students who teach other students. They lead discussions, seminars, and classes. It is a means by which Cuba solves the teacher shortage problem, and provides opportunities for active participation of students in the educational process.

From the start, the Cuban day-care movement encouraged close family-school relations to "unify the educational criteria and continue along a single path, thus avoiding a duality of directions for the child." [14] The círculos continually increased their educational role among parents, giving practical and theoretical structure to childhood development and methods of child rearing.

We believe that it is fundamental to get this information to the parents and to engage in close, systematic interchange with them, *en masse* as well as in small groups, in order to achieve total understanding of all fundamental aspects in the development of the individual, such as balanced diet, the conduct of adults where children are concerned, and adequate handling of individual problems. We believe that frequent communication is a permanent means of ongoing education and that it opens wide horizons in the quest for information. [15]

According to a Czech educator writing in *Simientes,* only the family "can give the child the best atmosphere for integral development." He goes on, "Socialist society considers the family as a fundamental element in the education of the child." [16]

Personal interviews, radio and television programs, and the publication of the monthly magazine *Simientes* have brought the day-care message to Cuban families. In one article, the author suggests that parents should consider the level of a child's development prior to giving him a specific toy, for often parents buy a toy for their child only to discover that he is totally uninterested in it, and that he prefers other things. "This occurs because we did not have the developmental stage of the child in mind when we chose it; we did not consider his level of maturity." The article goes on to explain in the simplest of terms what can be expected from children at various age levels and suggests appropriate playthings for children at each age. For example, before the age of one, "children are just 'trying out' the world; they begin to have their first contacts with their environment and need to understand it." Toys at this stage should "promote sensorial development, especially those of vision, hearing and tactile sensations." Playthings for this age should have bright colors, make sounds, move, and be easy to handle. As a word of caution to those parents who require further education, the article points out that toys should not have angles, sharp curves, or parts which come off easily. Also, since children at this age put everything in their mouths, paint should be nontoxic and the material from which the toys are made should be easily washable. For children under one year old, *Simientes* recommends rattles, dolls, and rubber toys, among other playthings. Simple guides are also offered for parents of older children.[17]

Many círculos maintain a bulletin board displaying child-guidance cards designed to educate parents on ways to develop proper affective relationships between them and their children. The cards also offer parents suitable approaches to assist the school in developing cognitive and motor skills. They are not unlike the suggestions in Chaim Ginott's *Between Parent and Child*.[18] One card advises parents on language development:

1. Take advantage of every opportunity to converse with your child. Let him talk freely and only intervene to stimulate his conversation.
2. Never make fun of what your child says because this might silence him.
3. Do not interrupt your child to correct errors in diction when he wants to talk because constant criticism is liable to inhibit his conduct. His errors should be corrected when he is not conversing and pronounces a word incorrectly or uses it incorrectly.
4. In order that your child speak correctly, you must also do so.

5. Each toy or new object that your child acquires or that can be directly used by him should provide him with new words. Take advantage of his interest to teach them to him.

6. Never make more than one correction at a time or be very insistent if the child shows some difficulty in articulating a certain sound. Be patient and he will overcome his difficulties.

The cards also offer suggestions to parents on how to deal with common behavioral patterns which might cause conflict at home. The following one proposes a method for dealing with restlessness:

If your child is very restless, is rarely calm, bullies his playmates, and hardly obeys commands, this means that your child is hyperactive, his system is dominated by excitative processes. To help him, you must recall and practice these suggestions:

1. Always keep him active. Give him toys appropriate for his age.

2. Give him the responsibility to carry out tasks which he can perform successfully.

3. Take him to parks and safe, open spaces as often as possible so that he may move and play freely.

4. Try to attend to him quickly at bath, meal, and nap time. It is very difficult for him to wait.

What you should *not* do with this child:

1. Let him remain inactive in the home trying to make him be still.

2. Scold him and continuously threaten him with stronger and stronger punishments.

3. Physically punish him.

4. Let him wait anxiously to carry out any activity: bath, meal, trips, etc.

Since January 1971 círculo parents' committees have been organized to offer wider home participation in the centers. Composed of parents, staff, and representatives from the Communist Party, Federation of Cuban Women, and the Cuban Pioneers' Union, the committees' tasks, as outlined in *Simientes*, are:

1. To provide a link between the círculos, parents, and the mass organization.
2. To get parents to participate in all the work required to improve and maintain an efficiently operating círculo which will endeavor to achieve a model círculo in the area.
3. To serve as the means—through bi-monthly educational talks and other avenues—of getting the message across to parents regarding the education of their children, thereby contributing to having the home continue the educational role performed by the círculo.[19]

From the círculos' point of view, parent cooperation is needed to insure that the children attend regularly, that they maintain adequate health and hygiene standards, and that parents offer their children the love and educational understanding necessary for the child's well-being. In addition, parents are enlisted to join maintenance teams to help in carpentry, painting, sewing, gardening, and other activities. Parents are also expected to contribute materials for toys and to participate in collective birthday parties.

Research in the United States on parent involvement in early-childhood programs reveals that when parents do participate, significant improvements in the children's education are achieved. These findings suggest that parents can help change and improve their own lives and the lives of their children by coordinating the efforts of the school and the home. As Merle Karnes, R. Reid Zehrbach, and James Teska of the University of Illinois propose: "Since the most important influences on the young child are his family members, it is only logical to enlist their aid in promoting his optimal environment." [20] Bronfenbrenner cautions, however:

The involvement of family members in the educational program of course poses a difficult dilemma to professional staff. On the one hand, there is a need to expose parents and other family members to new or different ways of dealing with their children. On the other hand, this must be done in such a way as to enhance, rather than lower, the power and prestige of these persons in the eyes of the child. [21]

Círculos also hold monthly meetings at which parents and staff have a chance to discuss such topics as diet, hygiene, health care, and suggested guidance methods.

A set of rigorous guidance cards, developed by the jardín psychology staff and the Ministry of Education, *Psychopedagogical Orientations: Your Child from Birth to Five Years*, is distributed to parents at meetings and at hospitals. [22] They set forth recommended child-rearing practices for parents. Clearly printed and well designed, each of the fifteen packets contains five to ten cards in sequence on a specific theme. Each card shows a child or a parent and child together illustrating a particular situation. Captions offer parents hints on what to do concerning various childhood experiences and involvements, and the backs of the cards provide detailed explanations on these themes:

The importance of the first year of the baby
Sucking is necessary for the infant
Crying
Home environment and love
Hygienic habits
Food
Play
Love, development, and learning
Egoism

Fear and shyness
Obedience
Punishment
Jealousy
Lying
First sexual manifestations in the child

An examination of the cards reveals a Dr. Spock-type approach, suggesting what should be emphasized and what should be avoided at different stages. The cards on sucking and toilet training urge that the child not be scolded for thumb sucking or bed wetting. Those on family environment for divorced or separated parents suggest that "the child must feel that separation is not a loss of love or attention from the parents."

The emphasis throughout is on building feelings of security and trust. The toilet-training guidelines, for example, urge parents not to compare their children with others; the cards on love, development, and learning encourage parents not to tease by calling their child ugly, his mother "old," or saying that his parents will go away. "The child does not understand that you are playing."

Focused on the building of parental attitudes that promote feelings of success rather than failure, the cards note that a child will not always succeed when trying something new, and that threatening and scolding in new situations will develop a resistance to learning. Indicating that proper parental behavior is a guide for children, the cards stress the importance of parental respect for their children, since "Sometimes children lack respect for elders because the elders lack respect for them." The Cuban cards outline these basic principles:

1. Through imitation and repetition in play, the child learns to live in the social world.

2. The way children play is always related to their age. Until eighteen months of age, play consists of touching, grabbing, throwing, squeezing, pulling, etc.

3. Until the age of four, the child is interested in playing with water, sand, clay, a wooden hammer, little machines, balls, and toy animals.

4. Until the age of three or four, the child likes to be in the company of other children, even though each one is playing by himself. After that, they play with each other.

5. At the age of three or four, playing of roles begins to predominate—playing of mother and father, doctor, teacher, etc.

6. At the age of seven, the child can already respect the rules of games. He prefers to play group games such as cops and robbers, hide and go seek, ball, etc.

According to these cards, "the child learns to live in the social world" through imitation and repetition of play. Reflecting the jardín philosophy, the emphasis is on "free play," "spontaneity," and "nature."

The cards make only passing reference to Cuba's societal goals, while focusing primarily on the child's individual ego development and personal habits. One notes that these sections on play show that this form of childhood activity is consistent with the goals of Cuba:

1. During the early years, good habits must be formed in children. For example, washing hands before meals, going to the bathroom in a certain place, not hitting other children, etc.

2. The child must begin to accept that some things are permitted and others prohibited (the socialization of the child).

3. The child will be subjected to the guidance of the adult in many of his daily activities, and will thus learn to obey. The child, by playing freely at what he wishes, does nothing that is in conflict with the principles of society. On the other hand, he learns to have initiative, to make decisions, to develop his imagination, etc.

4. During the first years, the child is not capable of understand-

ing the rules of games and needs to exert great effort to remain quiet and attentive.

As already noted, Cuba makes strong political attempts to fight "egoism" or selfishness and to develop a collective, socialist mentality. Cuban educators use the term "egoism" in a pejorative sense to describe the old regime's capitalist outlook. According to this view, money and the desire for it developed selfish attitudes in the pre-revolutionary society. As Castro cautions, in the new Cuba, "We cannot encourage or permit selfish attitudes among men if we don't want man to be guided by the instinct of selfishness, of individuality; by the wolf, by the beast instinct. . . . The concept of socialism and communism, the concept of higher society, implies a man devoid of these feelings." [23]

Interestingly, these child-rearing cards underscore the fact that egoism is normal in the first years of life, that it gradually disappears with healthy opportunities to play with other children, and that when a child exhibits a problem in sharing with other children, firm, fair adult leadership is necessary. The cards deal with selfishness in the following way:

Selfishness, in the two-to-four-year-old, is normal; but adequate treatment on the part of the parents will help him overcome it.

1. During the first years of life, because of his defenselessness and insecurity, the child is normally selfish, wanting everything for himself.

2. If the child is appropriately handled, his selfishness will gradually begin to disappear by the age of three or four.

3. Never tell or indicate to the child that he is selfish. Rather, praise and encourage his generous acts. More is gained with praise than with criticism.

4. The child who feels loved and is sure of it tends to be able to overcome his selfishness more easily.

5. When one sibling is jealous of another, his attitude should not be regarded as selfishness. At such times give him the affection that he desires, precisely so that he can overcome his selfishness.

Another card advises:

Allow your child to play in groups to help him overcome his selfishness.

1. Contact with other children and sharing of toys helps to overcome selfishness.

2. Jealousy and selfishness are related. Two sisters of about the same age should not always play alone together, since their continuous fights and quarrels over toys encourage their selfishness. It is good to have them play in groups.

3. The child who is alone with adults will be more selfish, since everything is always for him and he does not learn to share.

4. An only child will have more difficulty in overcoming his selfishness than one who has sisters and brothers, since he never has to share the affection of his parents, his toys, etc.

5. Some children have difficulty giving a toy to another child and so may cry when required to do so. If the child cries, it is good for him because he learns that sometimes he must yield. Tell him kindly, but firmly: "No, now it's the other child's turn; then it will be your turn again."

While they support an approach emphasizing psychological factors in child development, the cards recognize the importance of parental authority in defining limits of child behavior. In the cards on obedience, there are specific guidelines given for understanding the difference between constructive and blind obedience.

1. We can expect obedience in bathing habits, sleep and meal schedules, washing hands before eating, not touching other people's things without permission, not crossing streets alone until a certain age, and other situations.

2. As much as possible, leave to the child those decisions about things which do not greatly affect the organization of his daily life.

3. When you call him for some activity, give the child time to finish what he is doing.

The cards stress the child's need for "freedom and opportunity to decide matters." Parents' requests should not emphasize that "I" ask you to do something; parents should appeal to reason whenever possible. The cards encourage obedient children who follow routine and offer advice on how best to deal with children:

1. Don't shout. Maintain a firm but calm tone.

2. Speak civilly, demonstrating from the start that you believe the child will do what you request.

3. Don't expect blind obedience, because this will develop a useless person.

4. Children need freedom and opportunity to make decisions. They also need to obey.

5. Obedience is also necessary in order to help develop self-control.

6. Ask for things in an impersonal manner. One does not say, "You must go to school because I order you to go," but rather, "You must go to school because all the children of your age go to school in order to learn."

7. When authority among many persons—grandparents, aunts and uncles, etc.—is not united, not in agreement, it is not healthy for the development of the child.

The basic approach toward punishment is "keep your promise." If the parent does not intend to follow through, it is best not to threaten. The cards caution against corporal punishment. As with obedience, the suggestion is not to avoid all punishment, but to offer alternative approaches (such as explaining why one prohibits certain things).

1. Always fulfill your promises to your child; punishment is no exception.

2. Do not threaten punishments which you cannot fulfill.

3. Do not scold or threaten your child when you are going to punish him. Be firm, but calm. If he is under three, let your child cry when you forbid him something; he will understand. Between the ages of three and seven give an appropriate punishment that will help him to understand. For example: "Sit in that chair and think about why you shouldn't do that. When you are finished thinking come and tell me."

If the child is six years old or older, you can punish him by taking away outings, movies, etc. (but take care to punish the child on the same day as he committed his error).

In the end, the Cubans believe that the parental "model" affects the child; the cards propose that parents live according to the standards they set for their children:

1. Do not promise the child what you cannot fulfill.

2. If you do not do something because you are unable to do it, explain what happened.

3. Do not deceive your child by saying that you are not going to leave if you are thinking of leaving.

4. Do not say you are taking him to another place if you are taking him to the doctor.

5. Do not hide the death of someone in the family.

6. Do not involve the child in domestic problems.

As a further stimulus to wider parental and community involvement in the schools, the Cubans set up the *padrino* (godfather) system. Borrowed from Eastern European socialist countries, it is a cooperative arrangement between neighboring institutions and the schools. Padrino organizations agree to adopt a school in order to offer special services and assistance on a voluntary basis. Usually organized in factories, padrinos help with repairs, transportation, and arrangements for special occasions such as collective birthday parties. On a visit to one círculo I saw a truck pull up and a worker from a nearby padrino factory get out carrying materials to install a Mother Goose display in the waiting room. In another center, a padrino worker brought in a large birthday cake for a collective party. In a third, I overheard an asistente remind the director to call the padrino to repair a door. Simple outdoor play equipment—a seesaw and a crawl-through circular toy—was built for a jardín by a nearby construction materials plant which had taken the jardín under its wing. Padrinos who had "adopted" another school arranged for a caravan of cars and buses to take the children to a park.

On a strictly pragmatic basis, Cuban padrinos provide a variety of important services and repairs which would be difficult for a círculo to obtain, considering the current shortage of materials and skilled labor. Moreover, as a function of revolutionary education, padrinos serve to tie the school to the factory, providing children with practical, visual confirmation of workers and peasants as revolutionary altruists. Ultimately, the Revolution hopes that by seeing padrinos working to help maintain the círculo, the children will develop a profound respect for work.

The padrino system also reflects the revolutionary concern with education and the central position it holds. The Cubans take every opportunity to remind the people that the education of their children should be given top priority, even at the expense of work in the factories.

"The most important part of our work is human relations," commented the administrator of a Cuban refrigeration plant which had adopted a círculo as well as an elementary school. "We have come to know the children better and they have come to know us better. Most important is the personal and political relationships that exist between the workers and the school children." [24]

Padrinos usually affiliate themselves with centers at the request of the center director. Typically, a Party or union official is consulted, and if it is agreed that the request can be fulfilled, a decision is reached as to whether a man can be spared during working hours, or if a car is necessary, and so on. Depending on the call, padrinos either wait to caucus with administrators and party officials on what can be done, or, if there is a serious crisis, take prompt action.

One padrino member recalled that when the jardines were created, padrino aid was in great demand. His factory did all of the electrical installation, painted, cleaned the yard, installed a water pump, and gathered supplies.

Many padrinos invite the children into their factories, giving the youngsters guided tours, offering them candy, and working with them in the fields in agricultural labor brigades. Padrinos go so far as to visit families to discover why children are not attending class, encouraging parents to send their children to school by explaining the importance of education, discipline, and care.

The refrigeration-plant administrator summed up the notion of the "moral incentive" to work as a volunteer in the padrino system:

With our padrino system there is no monetary interest. Elsewhere one works because he is told to. Here we do the work voluntarily because we understand the children's need and because we like working with children. This creates a political atmosphere that an administrative brigade cannot. The way I see it, if our *compañeros*, the cane cutters, were offered a salary for cutting cane, fewer workers would go, and they would go under pressure. Nevertheless, they go regardless of wages. They go to work voluntarily because they are conscientious workers and they are aware of the need to cut the sugar cane. Comradeship exists between the voluntary cane cutters and the peasants. In the old days, they would work only for wages and would say, "It's my job; I work eight hours; I perform my duty or not, and after my eight hours, I go home." Here it's not that way at all. Here we tackle a task, be it the círculo or a school, until we are finished, because we are conscious of what we are doing.[25]

VI ★ CUBAN DAY CARE REVISITED

Circling over the José Martí airport, on my return visit to Cuba two years after my original year-long sojourn, I looked down over the lush green countryside and wondered what had really occurred in the two years since I had been there last. What was it really like now?

That question reminded me of the middle-aged taxi driver in Mexico City who, just a few days before, had taken me on one of my innumerable trips to locate the missing visa which would allow me entry into Cuba. When I arrived in Mexico City on my way to Havana from New York—a three-thousand-mile detour set up by international political roadblocks—I learned that my visa, which was supposed to have been waiting for me, had never arrived. It took almost two weeks of visits to the consul, long-distance calls to Havana to try to reach the Ministry of Education, which had invited me back to Cuba, and frustrating visits to the immigration offices, before the visa finally cleared. In one taxi ride, the driver, upon hearing about my forthcoming trip to Cuba, asked, "Mister, tell me, what is it really like? *¿Cuál es la realidad?*" He had heard so many conflicting stories about life on the island, both from exiles hostile to the country and from supporters, he hoped I could help to untie the cords of romance and hate entangling Cuba. His question stayed with me as I walked down the steps from the plane on to Cuban soil once again.

THE CHILDREN'S INSTITUTE

I soon learned that a major event in Cuban day care had occurred since my last visit. In mid-1971, President Osvaldo Dorticós Torrado had announced an altogether new approach to early-childhood education on the island, the creation of the Children's Institute.[1] Working on three fronts, the institute is to perform scientific research, supervise early-childhood educational institutions throughout the country, and attempt to raise the quality of day-care personnel.

Housed in a mansion previously occupied by one of the old, wealthy families of Havana, the institute has kept the original furnishings and uses the elegant, spacious rooms for offices and other functions. Quiet, except for occasional staff conferences, the mansion is more a base of operations than a working center. Research is conducted elsewhere, in classrooms and homes all over Cuba.

Dr. Daniel Alonso heads the research arm of the institute. A pediatrician previously associated with the Ministry of Public Health, he served as director of the William Solar Children's Hospital for two years and later was appointed chief of the medical section of MINSAP. He was responsible for postgraduate medical studies and more recently was in charge of the ministry's research programs. Alonso reported that the research projects under way at the new institute include studies on the child at birth, his physical growth and development, language expression during the first four years of life, the effects of early-childhood rearing in non-day-care families, parental attitudes toward child-rearing, and ways in which children adjust to elementary school. This last study will compare those children who have received day care with those who have come to grade school directly from the home. Inasmuch as most of the studies at the institute had just begun, no results were yet available.

According to Alonso, the most important study covers the physical growth of young people from birth to nineteen years of age. Fifty-six thousand youngsters from all regions, divided equally between boys and girls, will be measured to determine the growth patterns of fourteen physiological and anatomical features. "This study, of course, goes beyond the needs of the institute," Alonso noted. "But it could not stop at the age of five, since a young person normally grows until about twenty when his full skeletal development is achieved." [2] In addition to measuring height and weight, other, more complex biological growth characteristics will be studied. For example, 10 percent of the children in the national sample will be X-rayed to determine the bone development of their hands and wrists. A study to show the age-level when maturation is achieved will chart the appearance of secondary sex characteristics. At the same time, the height of the parents of the children in the sample will be measured to see whether they can predict the adult height of the children. Alonso noted that once a nation has been successful in decreasing its mortality rate, physical stature is an important indicator for measuring health standards. With the assistance of Dr. J. M. Tanner of London's Institute of Child Health, the national childhood growth project is scheduled to take three years to complete. The measurements themselves will be made over a two-year period, with the third year devoted to processing and evaluating the data. In the end, national tables will be published showing the results, which ultimately will serve as the basis for comparison with data to be compiled in a national study to be made in ten years.

The second major institute investigation gathers data on the health of children at birth, comparing a sample of infants born in Havana with a sample from rural, mountainous Oriente. The height, weight, maturation, period of gestation, and other indicators are correlated with physiological, maternal, and socioeconomic factors in the child's environment. By the fall of 1971, a study of 800 infants one month after birth had already been completed in Havana. Teams of research workers then traveled to the remotest and most underdeveloped regions of Oriente Province, where they are gathering comparative statistics on 1500 infants. The data from this project will be related to a number of child-care factors: hygiene, nursing, nutrition, preventive medicine, prenatal care, and others.

The institute also studies attitudes of mothers toward child rearing during the child's first three years, focusing particularly on those mothers who do not send their children to day-care centers. Alonso reports that sophisticated psychological testing, interviews, and surveys are being used in this study of a large sample of families from diverse socioeconomic strata in Havana. Still another study will compare attitudes toward child rearing on the part of parents with primary-school educations and parents with university degrees. Other projects are designed to gather data on reading and mathematical skills of four- and five-year-olds; a study of premature infants is yet to begin.

In an interview with Vilma Espín, the head of the Federation of Cuban Women, I learned why the Cubans undertook these massive national studies. Lamenting that at present Cubans work with standards set by research conducted in the United States, the Soviet Union, and Germany, she indicated that the lack of Cuban norms prevented the nation from charting its progress in early-childhood education, health, and other programs. With more than fifty thousand children in day care, the studies will concentrate on large enough samples to develop a table of normal development for the average Cuban child.

Espín noted that in addition to the research being conducted by the new institute, other aspects of childhood development and health standards are being studied by MINSAP. For example, in cooperation with the institute, the ministry is conducting a study of childhood speech and hearing disorders to determine the number of children suffering from these malfunctions, and to attempt to understand their origins. Espín reiterated that the focus is on the first years of life. "It is in these first six years that man develops physically, mentally, psychologically, and socially." [3]

In the area of public health, the institute sees itself as moving from the immediate goals of the first decade of the Revolution—such as the reduction of infant mortality—to new areas of preventive medicine. Even though public health officials such as Alonso do not feel that infant mortality has reached its minimum level, they consider it to have been reduced to an acceptable level.* The 1980 goal is set at only twenty deaths per thousand live births.[4] To achieve this, a massive program of prevention is under way, enlisting not only Cuba's medical personnel but experts from other sectors, including educators, sociologists, psychologists, biostatisticians, and anthropologists.

In addition to MINSAP, other national agencies also lend their support to the institute; these include, among others, the Ministry of Education, the University of Havana, the Academy of Sciences, and Cuba's Central Planning Board. Alonso characterized the institute as "a multidisciplinary institute whose fundamental purpose is to study the growth and development of the child in our country during the first five years of life, the preschool age." [5]

During my conversations with early-childhood educators and institute officials, I wondered why the Cubans felt the need to organize such a prodigious research effort at that time. In addition, why hadn't they placed it under the auspices of the University of Havana or some leading hospital with the tradition and facilities available for research? From what I gathered, they felt that they were unprepared for it earlier, that their educational establishment was not

* The infant mortality rate in 1968 was 37.4 deaths per thousand.

quite ready. Before 1971, they had channeled their efforts into opening day-care centers, securing staff, designing health procedures, organizing food and clothing distribution, offering in-service training, and developing effective liaison with physicians, nurses, nutritionists, and other specialists. These efforts were essential. Once day care began to work, it was time to evaluate critically the program's methods, procedures, and designs, and its effects on children and society alike. The past twelve years have seen the building of a day-care machine from scratch. Apparently in 1971 the time had come to consider the effectiveness of the programs and appropriate plans for the future.

The institute itself is under the direction of the Federation of Cuban Women. The FMC was selected from among other possible agencies, because it had had the longest and most fruitful experience in working with children. As noted earlier, the FMC had the responsibility for all day care from the very beginning. Alonso also indicated that, "in addition, we needed the cooperation in many of our projects of the great mass of women who made up the Federation's membership." Fully aware of the unique alliance between a mass political organization and a scientific and technical effort such as the institute, the Cubans believe that because of the massive support needed for the institute's projects, the FMC would prove a perfect home. Alonso supported this notion:

I can't predict the future, but at this moment the decision to place it under the Federation was very wise because the basic resource that our work needs at this point is the massive cooperation of our people, massive participation—especially of our women—to transport children from here to there, attend to them, help them, visit them. All of this is vastly facilitated when we have the collaboration of the popular organization most directly in contact with the children.[6]

THE END OF THE JARDINES

In addition to Vilma Espín, who chairs the governing council of the institute, other members of the council include Clementina Serra, director of the círculos, and Consuelo Miranda, head of the educational training programs. Lela Sánchez and Haydée Salas, who created the jardines, are conspicuously missing from among the leaders of the new "unified" early-childhood education organization. Under the plan to centralize all preschool care, the institute took charge of all the scattered early-childhood programs, including the círculos, the jardines, and "whatever other groups involve themselves in the care of the child of preschool age." [7] What had previously been a decentralized effort was now replaced by strong central control.

The new position holds that the jardín and the círculo were not fundamentally incompatible, and that a centralized system is simply a recognition of the fact that both day-care services were striving toward the same goals. Alonso argued that "the difference in philosophy was always more illusory than real." Noting that there were different methodological approaches and that each day-care route had separate characteristics all its own, he made it clear that from his perspective there was no basic disagreement on the "conceptual and philosophical questions as to how to guide the child." [8] Dismissing the difficulties involved in integrating the two systems, Alonso emphasized, "The jardines left the child with almost total liberty of action while the círculos maintained certain norms of discipline. But the differences were not great." [9] From my own observations, it seemed to me that he was seriously minimizing the very great differences between the two philosophies.

As late as the fall of 1971, despite the pronouncements at the top calling for full integration into a unified day-care system, the jardines continued as they had before—even though the former jardín leadership was working in other areas. Miranda explained:

> At this moment, the jardines continue to function exactly as before. Later, it will be necessary to see what we can do to unify the programs. All of the day-care institutions are now unified under the Instituto de la Infancia, but the jardines are not under the círculos; they are still called jardines. What interests us is to give the maximum possible service and attention to the child.[10]

Unification tends to blur ideological differences in the service of consensus. In the end, the jardín philosophical position will hardly be acknowledged by early-childhood educators. If the institute had allowed the jardín cadre a voice in the new system, perhaps there might have been a chance for the competing advocates to argue their separate concepts; but with the dismissal of the jardín leadership there appears to be little chance for their position to be attended to in the councils.

Nonetheless, the Cubans believe that a proper hearing will be given to alternative approaches. Alonso has predicted that as time goes on all points of view will be aired "with absolute liberty of discussion." Yet despite the optimistic outlook, Alonso dismissed the notion that any radical departures from current plans would be entertained. "In the final analysis," Alonso concluded, "the subtleties of child care depend much less on the norm that may or may not have been established than on the individual interpretation of the norm by the person directly in charge of an institution. The care a child receives depends on so many subtle factors." [11]

As we have already seen, these subtle differences, according to jardín philosophy, are critical. If the jardín approach is to be submerged by the círculos, then the "spontaneous" day care offered by the jardín will not be part of the future of Cuban early-childhood education.

In a final visit to a jardín during the fall of 1971 I interviewed the staff once again and discovered, not surprisingly, that the personnel, although continuing for the time being in the same tradition as before, saw the handwriting on the wall and lamented the coming dissolution of their schools. I spoke with one of the women who was among the first to have worked with children under free-play conditions. She was unsympathetic to the institute's new directions. She insisted that the jardín strengths—warmth and feeling for the children, inter-aging, and spontaneity—were still valid and needed continued support. In short, she advocated the original jardín philosophy as the best way of educating and rearing children. In the long run she believed that the jardín approach would be vindicated, that children do better in school if they are permitted to play freely, that older children have an important role to play in the maturation process of their younger schoolmates, and that child-developed play was as valuable as adult-imposed activities, if not more so. Recalling the early days and the cooperative efforts to organize her jardín, she said sadly, "We brought liters of sand to fill in and to provide a play area, working together with volunteer parents to build a jardín." [12]

When asked whether she felt that the jardín approach would be lost in its merger with other organizations under the aegis of the institute, Lela Sánchez replied:

The experience is not a loss—we have not lost the children with whom we worked. Also, there is a staff that has been trained using our standards. Now the institute has an opportunity to study our methods in practice. We have not wasted our efforts since our personnel are left with certain attitudes and standards and are now distributed throughout Cuban day care. And the bonds we made working together in theory and practice will not be lost in the institute. Aside from this is the simple fact that what we are dealing with are not problems unique to our jardines, but our problems are those of the entire community.[13]

Relieved of her duties in early-childhood education, Sánchez was at work on a unique housing plan which enlisted the talents of the workers in the factories in designing and building their own homes. While those with such skills as carpentry, plumbing, and electrical work were taken off their factory jobs to work on creating housing for themselves and the rest of the workers in the plant, the rest doubled their efforts in order to permit the construction brigade to complete its work.

Still committed to the jardín position, Sánchez understood the political realities that took her away from her work with children. When I admired her passion for her work, she pointed out the critical difference between passion and love for a cause:

There is a difference between passion and love. Passion for work hinders objectivity. Love is positive; when love becomes passion it is negative. It is very important to love what you are doing, but when it converts to passion, it is dangerous. And this is the negative element which Haydée and I both have. To be a real scientist one must function with a great deal of caution and with as much determination as an elephant. One must be realistic. Those of us who are not scientists often become impassioned. One minute we are positive, then suddenly we are negative. Thus, it is very useful to create the Children's Institute, so that all will be unified and there can be a scientific base for all this work.[14]

The "merger" of the jardines with the círculos raises some rather fundamental issues for Cuba. The loss of the jardín itself is not disturbing because it was an educational panacea. But some of the elements of the jardín atmosphere require further study and experimentation before they are completely abandoned by Cuban day care. The end of the jardines means the demise of a certain degree of flexibility, a spirit which the círculos seem unable to manage. Interaging, for example, appears to be a direction the círculos ought to explore. It is an idea that the British have accepted on a wide scale and have even expanded into elementary school, and it is an approach that appears to have decided benefits on all levels of schooling.[15] Also, for parents to be able to drop off their children when convenient and pick them up at the end of the day, with no rigid schedule to adhere to, seems to relieve some of the tensions inherent in the school-home transition.

Granted, the jardines may have failed to concentrate their energies on children who did not come from professional and former middle-class homes. While the permissive atmosphere may have suited these particular children, it may not be appropriate for the majority of Cuban children. Most Cuban families gladly send their children to a place where cleanliness and order are essential features of day care. In discussions about the jardines with the círculo leadership, I learned that the kind of education that most Cubans want for their children is not satisfied by the jardín. The círculo view has it that large masses of Cuban children would not have proper diets, learn socially acceptable habits, or come in contact with art, music, and books were it not for the kind of approach followed by the círculos. While free play may fill the needs of children from culturally endowed homes, it cannot substitute for the massive re-education the círculos feel they must offer the children of Cuba.

Nevertheless, many aspects of the jardines showed a concern for the *child* in childhood, and Cuban day care without the jardines may foreclose this approach in the círculos.

The impression left by the merger may be that the jardines failed altogether.

ESCUELA DE EDUCADORAS

Under the new organization, the Children's Institute is also responsible for staff and in-service training. A complete revamping of the teacher-training program covers "cultural" subjects, professional preparation, a planned sequential four-year program, higher admission standards, and a university-trained faculty. In short, the new direction calls for a more highly trained staff than was possible at the outset of Cuban day care. The new course is called Escuela de Educadoras (School for Educators) whose graduates will be called "educadoras" and not asistentes. The shift in training emphasis from paraprofessional to professional status is reflected in the more professional title, "educadora." Nonetheless, one must remember that even after intensive training, Cuban day-care workers have only the equivalent of a high school diploma.

Much of the desire among the educational leadership to increase the level of education of day-care workers comes from their increased sensitivity to the child's needs for adults who understand the world in more sophisticated ways. Vilma Espín declared:

We want the preschool-age child to receive an explanation for every question and that such an explanation be both truthful and on his level of comprehension. Naturally, the personnel must be trained in the fundamental concepts of many things: mathematics, physics, chemistry, etc. We want certain basic concepts well understood by our day-care personnel and we want them to know how to explain what they know to the children. When a child wants to know why a shower has water and where it comes from, the women should know enough about it to explain it simply. And when a child wants to know what that cloud is above the pot of boiling water, the worker should be able to explain the concept of water vapor simply and comprehensibly. In other words, we don't want the children to be miseducated by superstition, old wives' tales, or fantasy in place of fact. We want our children to be inquisitive, to be acquainted with nature from the moment they ask their first questions.[16]

Inasmuch as the training institute entered on its new path only recently, published materials on its operations are not yet available: much of the curriculum designed to train day-care workers is still in the formative stages. For teacher-training institutions in other countries and for local communities starting day-care programs, the Cuban training model is of special interest because it builds upon a decade of experience. From talks with Miranda and her colleagues I have synthesized the goals of day-care training into a ten-point program:

1. *Liberal arts and psychopedagogical skills.* To qualify as an educadora, those working with children should be trained in "cultural" subjects as well as educational psychology.

2. *Physical and hygienic tasks.* Educadoras must understand that such activities as bathing, feeding, and napping are an integral part of day care. Since the young child's day includes these routines, much of his learning experiences occur at these times. The educadora who views these chores as separate from her professional duties has not grasped the nature of the child's needs and her professional response to them.

3. *Recruitment.* Recruiting young people into the early-childhood training program requires the full cooperation of

sister agencies such as the Ministry of Education, which supports the efforts of the institute by publicizing the role of educadoras. To this end, students are invited to visit day-care centers and spend time with the children and the staff.

4. *Screening and selection.* To determine whether a particular student has the calling for work with children in day-care centers, initial screening by the institute and field placement staff must help to identify those personalities that cannot be expected to act in the child's best interest. Since screening is an ongoing process of selection, the School of Psychology of the University of Havana has been called upon to find ways of measuring "positive" personalities so that these students will be encouraged to continue working with young children.

5. *The day-care center as a training institution.* The training school should not be the only locus of training; the day-care center itself plays a critical role. Círculo directors must be skilled in training new students and, in turn, students must be given major responsibility for the children in the classroom. While they are in training, under the supervision of established day-care workers and directors, the experienced gained from work in the classroom acts as a basis for discussion in the training institute.

6. *Reliance on youth.* Emphasizing the need for young people in early-childhood education, the school for educators encourages sixteen-year-olds to qualify. Even fourteen- and fifteen-year-olds are accepted, and the maximum age has been reduced from thirty to twenty-five.

7. *Early practice.* An early introduction into the classroom not only "bridges the gap between theory and practice," as the Cubans are fond of saying, but helps students at an early stage to clarify whether or not they are suited for this kind of work.

8. *In-service training.* In addition to training novice day-care workers, the institute is also responsible for in-service training. In line with this aim, directed study programs call on the school's training faculty to leave the institute every two weeks to participate in ongoing círculo activities.

9. *Boarding.* Training institutes usually provide boarding facilities for educadoras-in-training. The boarding-school atmosphere offers intensive study plus collective living. Food, clothing, and board are all given to the students without charge. For in-service personnel, boarding is available several weeks a year.

10. *Small scale.* Rather than bury students in a massive program, the training institute consciously opted for limited enrollment. In order to come to grips with the continuous need for careful supervision, intimate faculty-student contact, and maintenance of quality, the small scale offers Cuban day-care training a carefully coordinated project for the future.

NATIONAL CONGRESS OF EDUCATION AND CULTURE

Perhaps the most striking development in day care and general educational circles since my last visit to Cuba came about at the National Congress of Education and Culture held in Havana, April 23–30, 1971. Nearly 1800 delegates from all over the country attended. The Cuban press gave it full coverage. Experts from the Ministry of Education and the congress participated in panels on nationally broadcast television to discuss and interpret the sessions.

The seven-day congress was attended by 1781 delegates. More than 400 papers and 3106 recommendations were presented.[17] From my conversations with ministry personnel and teachers I perceived an excitement, involvement, and hope for change that emanated from this congress. Even a worker who was disturbed by Cuba's economic problems and shortages said, "One area where I really think we're breaking through, where we're really looking to what the grass-roots level is saying, is education. Teachers were able to speak up, to get grievances off their chests, and follow the proposals up to and through the congress." [18]

During the months before the congress more than 116,000 educational workers attended 2599 sessions at the municipal, regional, and provincial level to discuss seven major themes:

Formation of the student.
The educational worker and his role in education.
Objectives and content of education.
Methods, means, and evaluation of teaching.
School organization and administration.
Influence of the social environment on education.
Popular agencies of education.[19]

The leadership apparently went to great lengths at the congress to involve large numbers of classroom teachers in planning, discussions, and recommendations. To some extent, the many local meetings that were held preceding the congress served to give expression to the views of the educational workers at the local level. In effect, it was an attempt to move toward a non-elitist approach.

Early-childhood programs were affected by the congress in a number of ways. One major recommendation proposed a comprehensive, cumulative record for all students in the system, one designed to guide teachers and other personnel with respect to the total educational life of each child. While a copy of the standard record card was not yet available before my departure, the proposal did indicate that the card would begin with a record of the child's educational achievement in preschool programs and continue through the university.[20]

Most Cuban teachers and administrators were excited about having complete personality and academic data available on each student. They said it would help them carry out improved guidance. In other parts of the world, detailed record keeping and teacher comments have often led to the dangerous path of teachers' self-fulfilling prophesies, of typing students, of limiting rather than extending student horizons. Cubans must ask themselves whether the benefits they seek from that grand cumulative folder will ultimately be defeated by trapping their students between their covers.

The congress reaffirmed the belief in several trends in Cuban day care. Among these were the continued support of the family as the best environment for the young child, continued support for coeducation in early-childhood programs as well as in later years, further recognition of the need for the padrino system, and the support of mass organizations.[21]

Rank-and-file teachers criticized Cuban day care for the paucity of children's literature, including picture books, for classroom use.

The congress proclaimed itself in favor of giving greater urgency to children's literature, a search for new elements of narrative and illustrative language, and a better use of resources that until now have been devoted to older children and adolescents. Development of imaginative and creative abilities in children, the development of their aesthetic tastes and reading habits, contribute to placing them in contact with reality in many areas according to their age and school level.[22]

Resolutions adopted by the congress implied that Cuban writers were at fault for not providing sufficient materials;

they had not applied themselves to the task. But from one writer's perspective it appeared otherwise:

If I had been at that session I would have stood up and said, "True, we don't have many writers involved with children's books and songs, but the problem is not so much with writers as much as with publishers." For example, there are writers who have written many children's books or songs; but the important thing is to give them the opportunity to print what they have and to make it available. The congress is right in saying that there is a lack of these materials, but one must be willing to place a value on it. In my opinion, if the publishing industry placed a higher value on such books, we would have them.[23]

In her report to the congress, Clementina Serra indicated that while the círculos appeared to be doing a good job at developing the mental and physical capacities of the child, shortages in furniture, materials, and other equipment prevented them from achieving outstanding records.

Criticism was leveled at the Cuban mass media for not providing adequate educational programs on television and in other areas of mass communication. Concerned with the deleterious effects of U.S. animated films and old foreign movies still shown on Cuban television, teachers and experts alike agreed that the values portrayed in these films went counter to those attitudes found acceptable by Cuba's educational system. Many educators were disturbed to learn that in many círculos the television set was turned on during lunch or at other times during the day; the day-care center was, in effect, a silent partner to the events on the screen. Calling for a reassessment of mass communication, the congress declared:

Mass media are powerful tools for ideological formation. They help develop social consciousness and their use and development should not be the result of chance improvisation or spontaneity. There is a need for closer ties between the Ministry of Education and the appropriate agencies which prepare programs for radio, TV, and movies, newspaper articles, and literary and artistic works which will contribute effectively to the formation of children and adolescents. . . . It was suggested that the media be more careful with its use of vocabulary, scenes and labels that affect the instruction and formation of pupils negatively, and that a careful review be made of programs which might develop in the child erroneous and deformed ideas concerning courage, skill, love, and work.[24]

The congress also supported a more intense effort to educate Cuban children in the traditions of Latin American culture, "centering our efforts in art and literature on the development of our own cultural forms and values, on the development of our knowledge of the cultural values of the fraternal peoples of Latin America and on the assimilation of the best that universal culture offers, without its being imposed upon us from abroad." [25]

Although it pointed toward some new directions in the educational life of Cuba, the congress did not alter its long-range goals. While some tactics may have changed, and other concerns may have intensified, the essentials of Cuban early-childhood philosophy remain the same. When I asked Cubans whether they felt that the congress had altered the goals of their educational system, most indicated that while it had deepened their sense of awareness or commitment, it had not fundamentally transformed their aims. One educator, Max Figueroa Araujo, the general director of the Center of Education and Development at the Ministry of Education, recalled Cuba's revolutionary idealism:

I don't think our objectives have changed. The objectives have been extended, enriched, and clarified as a result of our experiences. The objectives for us are very clear: we want to attain a society that satisfies all of the material needs of our people without forgetting that there are other needs—the conscience of men. We have to pursue the social consciousness of our people simultaneously with our struggle against underdevelopment. We want men who feel themselves part of humanity, who are prepared to struggle to achieve the well-being of all men, who suffer with the suffering of other peoples and rejoice in their good fortune. Naturally, the objective is one thing and experience itself is, at times, another. By that I mean, we're always going to face practical problems in achieving our aims.[26]

¿CUAL ES LA REALIDAD?

The reality for Cuban early-childhood education today is part of Cuba's climate, its people, its hardships, and most importantly, its Revolution. Cuba is a lovely garden of an island, and its people are a special variety of flower, remarkably enthusiastic about their country and their blossoming children.

Pampered—in the best sense of that word—their children are loved, cared for, well-fed, the *queridos* of the Revolution. Love, joy, enthusiasm—all very Cuban. All have much to do with the Revolution and its expression in early-childhood education. One is repeatedly struck by the tenderness and warmth shown by many of those who work in the schools, and surprised by the dedication of many staff members—from the asistentes in the centers to the educational leadership.

Cuba's climate, natural beauty, and special brand of people all contribute to making her unique. Its Revolution, too, is different. As Richard Fagen has noted, "both the enemies and friends of the revolution have failed to appreciate how profoundly revolutionary programs have been conditioned and shaped by a series of factors that are peculiarly Cuban, factors which set the island apart." [27]

With the coming of the Revolution, the Cubans faced many immediate economic and social problems which threatened to smash it into shards. Were it not for the revolutionary idealism fired by Fidel Castro, together with the national dream of a glorious day ahead, the Revolution certainly would not have survived the decade. Chief among the goals staunchly supported by the Revolution in the early days, and even later, as it progressed into the 1970s, was the insistence on massive educational support. Consider only the dramatic 1961 campaign against illiteracy which dominated the island, despite the Bay of Pigs invasion and massive social and economic changes. It had mobilized more than 200,000 young people who went into the mountains, the outlying regions, and all over the island, to teach the illiterate campesino. By the end of 1961, official figures showed that 707,000 Cubans had learned the first steps of reading and writing (first-grade level was achieved). Day care is part of that continuing Cuban effort to educate its population. For Castro, revolution and education are the same thing.

Only a revolution is capable of totally changing the educational scene in a country, because it also totally changes the political scene, the economic scene, and the social scene. The levels of ignorance and illiteracy, the numbers of children not attending school are really frightening in the economically exploited nations. Why? . . . Because in reality there is not the least interest in remedying these conditions.[28]

While insisting on massive educational support, Cuba still faces many critical problems. Shortages of essential goods make classroom materials scarce; the lack of a well-trained, professional staff of educators, teachers, and administrators forces the Cubans to rely on less than the best personnel; the Batista legacy of exploitation and poverty often cripples their attempts to move faster; and those elements sown by the Revolution itself—bureaucracy, inefficiency, dogmatism, parochialism—hamper its own efforts.

With such formidable difficulties, Cuba's commitment of its resources and political leadership to education in general and day-care programs in particular is most impressive. Lacking official figures, it is difficult to translate this commitment into financial terms. Extrapolating the possible cost of the Cuban effort from the available Head Start data, the financial resources that seem to have gone into the Cuban program are enormous. In the United States, the cost per child in Head Start is $1000, not including capital construction. Basing our estimate on the U.S. figures, the Cubans spend fifty million dollars a year to support the fifty thousand children in the círculos. Undoubtedly the cost of the círculo operation is even higher than that if one adds medical services, uniforms, food, and infant care. Viewed as a whole, including the cost of buildings and supporting staff (psychologists, administrators, curriculum planning and development personnel), Cuba must spend more of a percentage of its gross national product on day care than most countries in the world. In the United States, for example, only six states provide some form of support for pre-kindergarten programs, and only eight states order school districts to offer kindergarten to all who want it.[29]

The other positive features of the Cuban day-care system are also to be applauded. In the continuity of its early-childhood education, Cuba has broken down the artificial separations that split infant care from nursery school, and nursery school from kindergarten. By using the Federation of Cuban Women as the umbrella agency for all preschool programs, they have effectively cut through the bureaucratic red tape which afflicts early-childhood education in most other countries, where infant care is left to a public health authority, care for nursery-school age children switched to another agency, and finally, kindergartners are handed over to a ministry or board of education. Moreover, as a mass women's organization, the FMC acts to strengthen community involvement with the children by taking over the responsibility of child care from remote bureaucracies. In addition, FMC sponsorship assists one of the principal aims of child-care programs—the integration of women into the broader economic and social fabric of the nation.

Other things also broaden the educational participation of the people. For the most part, racial integration is assured by Cuban institutions, which not only prohibit racism but have eliminated the economic basis for discrimination to the point at which it has been so severely curtailed that a visitor finds it practically impossible to detect, if it exists at all. With no private day-care centers nor special exclusionary schools, children of the political leadership, ministers, industrial managers, and party officials attend the same centers as all the other children in their locality.

While the destruction of the old society offers the potential for growth and development, it does not guarantee the elimination of some of the spirit of the past. Often, a naïve, an almost primitive misunderstanding of the goals of the Revolution prevents the Cubans from breathing the kind of liberated atmosphere Che dreamed about. One is both amused and saddened by the sounds of teachers attempting to develop new Cuban men with cheerleader shouts of "F-I-D-E-L" or catechism-like *lemas*—slogans—glorifying the Revolution.

It is to Cuba's credit that it often recognizes the simple-mindedness of some classroom methods. In conversations with experts in curriculum development and change, I found many to be sensitive to the limited capacities of the paraprofessional staff. The leadership understands that much of the staff has minimal educational experience and that it is unrealistic to expect asistentes who have a sixth-grade education to perform with the same kind of skill and sensitivity as those who have gone through more rigorous training. Experiments are now under way to determine what kinds of curricula are appropriate for use in the classroom by unskilled child-care workers.[30] The Children's Institute will study whether or not curriculum plans were drawn up in a vacuum, without an appreciation of the ability of the asistente to translate the activities indicated into classroom practice. These curriculum plans will be tested and examined in order to reach decisions on the future of the day-care program.

One is always aware of the enormous task of upgrading day-care workers through training and continuing education programs. Recent developments in technology will make it possible for Cuban asistentes to receive additional training through cassette tape recordings and other audio-visual devices. In music education, which was strongly encouraged by the congress, archival recordings of children's songs and the Cuban musical heritage can not only provide classroom materials but offer the mass communication industry a fund from which to draw.

As has been discussed earlier, the círculos want their children to learn all sorts of things at very young ages. But I am unimpressed with Cuba's ability to teach four- and five-year-olds to read; I fail to understand the pressing need to train little children to jump through reading hoops at age four. If children can learn to read at four, does that mean that day care should expend its educational energies that way? The question should be: Is reading an appropriate developmental goal for that age? Should these children be spending their time playing, constructing, discovering, and relating to each other and their adult leaders in positive, reinforcing ways? Or should they be decoding vowels, syllables, and words? In short, the mere demonstration that something can be learned at an early age does not necessarily mean that this learning experience is a positive step in the child's educational and emotional development. In the long run, only extended research will be able to deal with this aspect of learning; in the meantime, I question the value of training children to perform sanctified adult learning rituals.

In context, however, Cuba's ostensibly heavy concentration on the achievement of skills at a very early age is not as demanding of the child as it would seem from an inspection of the syllabus. While they have provided specific objectives in vocabulary, language, and socialization in the spirit of the new Cuban man, the "directed" activities were never meant to consume the child's full day at the círculo. Most schools find that the suggested learning program can be slipped in at appropriate moments during the rest of the day's routine. Bathing, play, eating, napping, and all the other pressing demands of the círculo schedule prevent the day-care center from turning directed learning into an *idée fixe*.

Probably one of the most serious problems facing the círculos in the context of their directed-learning programs, as well as in their other activities, is the extremely poor educational materials available and the scarcity of creative ideas in this area. Rarely does one find an asistente or a director who understands the infinite possibilities of abandoned industrial supplies, scraps, and odds and ends as effective classroom materials. While it is true that Cuba's economic situation prevents it from indulging children with expensive toys, Cuban educators seem to lack experience in the use of materials which early-childhood educators practically everywhere else have found to be essential ingredients of creative activities. Perhaps the new *talleres,* or shops, which have been set up in each region, and where teachers learn to produce puzzles and other teaching aids, will push the círculos in a more creative direction.

Aware of their shortcomings, the Cubans invite early-childhood educators from abroad to hold workshops for asistentes on techniques and activities. During the summer of 1970, for example, a group of French art educators worked with the círculo staff; the Boston Teaching Project, comprised of a number of young U.S. teachers, also visited Cuba recently and offered workshops on several techniques in "open education." Naturally, continued interchange of approaches and methods will permit the Cubans to become more sophisticated. While Cuba has much to learn from the experiences of foreign educators who have come to accept a more relaxed and open approach to young children and their education, much of the rest of the world can profit from the Cuban effort. Their basic understanding of children's need for proper nutrition and comprehensive medical care, their fantastic support for a universal and free system offering child care from forty-five days to five years of age under a single administration, their insistence on parental and community involvement—these and other startling successes offer evidence of what is possible in the education of the very young.

INTRODUCTION

[1] Richard R. Fagen, *The Transformation of Political Culture in Cuba* (Stanford: Stanford University Press, 1969), p. 15.

[2] *Ibid.*, p. 3.

I. GOALS

[1] Wyatt MacGaffey and Clifford R. Barnett, *Cuba: Its People, Its Society, Its Culture* (New Haven: Human Relations Area Files Press, 1962), pp. 142, 343–344.

[2] Interview with Inez Orfano, Havana, 1969.

[3] Susan Kaufman Purcell, "Modernizing Women for a Modern Society: The Cuban Case" (Paper delivered at meeting of the Latin American Studies Association, Austin, Texas, Dec. 3–4, 1971), p. 4.

[4] *Ibid.*, p. 5; see also Lowry Nelson, *Rural Cuba* (Minneapolis: University of Minnesota Press, 1950), p. 133, and MacGaffey and Barnett, *Cuba*, p. 54.

[5] Fidel Castro, Speech delivered at Santa Clara, Dec. 9, 1966, in Linda Jenness, *Women and the Cuban Revolution* (New York: Pathfinder Press, 1970), p. 5.

[6] Fidel Castro, Speech delivered on May 1, 1966, in Martin Kenner and James Petras, eds., *Fidel Speaks* (New York: Grove Press, 1969), p. 187.

[7] Clementina Serra, "Report on the Círculos Infantiles," typewritten (July 13, 1969), p. 1.

[8] Castro, Speech delivered on May 1, 1966, in Kenner and Petras, eds., *Fidel Speaks*, p. 188.

[9] In 1964, only 282,069 women were gainfully employed in all of Cuba. By 1970 the number of women in the labor force was nearly 600,000. The most recently announced goal of the FMC—incorporating another 100,000 women into the labor force during 1971—indicates that the FMC has no intention of diminishing its efforts of the past few years. Purcell, "Modernizing Women," p. 15.

These figures do not include the thousands of women who volunteer each week to do agricultural and other work for the Revolution. For example, during my 1971 visit there were hundreds of Cubans volunteering each evening and weekend to enlarge the sports stadium in Havana. These volunteer women, from households, offices, and factories, worked side by side with men to complete the stadium in time for the next international sports competition. See Ana Ramos, "La mujer y la revolución en Cuba," *Casa de las Américas*, XI: 65–66 (1971), pp. 56–72, for a recent report on women in the Cuban economy and education.

10 Elizabeth Sutherland, *The Youngest Revolution: A Personal Report on Cuba* (New York: Dial Press, 1969), pp. 174–175. See also Roberta Alper, "Revolution and Feminism: Women in Cuba" (Paper delivered at meeting of the Latin American Studies Association, Austin, Texas, Dec. 3–4, 1971) for an analysis of women's liberation in Cuba with reference to two contemporary novels. Alper points out that the right to work for Cuba is the key to fundamental change for women in Cuban society. She notes: "By living and actively participating in a society where unalienated labor exists, Cuban women have the best conditions imaginable for the development of the kind of self-respect and dignity that is the groundwork for other levels of liberation. The right of women to engage in work valued by the economy does not, of course, involve as a necessary corollary instantaneous abolition of the "double standard" in sexual mores nor the immediate questioning of the nuclear family or the automatic eradication of the passive female. What it does do, however, is help create human beings who will have the strength and confidence to deal with these questions." *Ibid.*, pp. 9–10.

Both the Purcell paper and the Alper papers will appear in a forthcoming collection on women in Latin America to be published by the University of Pittsburgh Press: Ann Pescatello, ed., *Female and Male in Latin America*.

11 Purcell, "*Modernizing Women*," pp. 17–18.

12 *Ibid.*, pp. 18–19.

13 Serra, "Report on the Círculos Infantiles," pp. 8–10.

14 For an analysis of Cuban revolutionary ideology in the schools in general, see Gerald H. Read, "The Cuban Revolution-

ary Offensive in Education," *Comparative Education Review*, XIV:2 (June, 1970), pp. 131–143.

[15] Joseph Kahl, "The Moral Economy of a Revolutionary Society," *Transaction*, April, 1969, p. 32.

[16] Fidel Castro, Speech at Las Villas on the 15th anniversary of the attack on the Moncada, *Granma Weekly Review*, July 26, 1968, pp. 3–5.

[17] For a particularly trenchant analysis of this concept, see Richard R. Fagen, *The Transformation of Political Culture in Cuba* (Stanford: Stanford University Press, 1969).

[18] Theodore Hsi-en Chen, "The New Socialist Man," *Comparative Education Review* XIII:1 (Feb. 1969), p. 88.

[19] Karl Marx, "Economic and Philosophical Manuscripts," in Erich Fromm, *Marx's Concept of Man* (New York: Frederick Ungar Publishing Company, 1961).

[20] Read, "Cuban Revolutionary Offensive," p. 135.

[21] Nancy Garrity, "Cuba as a Case Study: The Role Played by Education in the Socialization of the New Man" (M.A. thesis, Tufts University, 1971), p. 27; see also Kenner and Petras, eds., *Fidel Speaks*, and John Gerassi, ed., *Venceremos!: The Speeches and Writings of Ernesto Che Guevara* (New York: The Macmillan Company, 1968).

[22] Marta Santander and Consuelo Miranda, "Círculos infantiles: la educación en la edad temprana," in *Seminario interdisciplinario de educación permanente*, mimeographed (Havana, 1970), p. 4.

[23] For a rigorous analysis and report on the theme of "moral" versus "material" incentive, see Bertram Silverman, *Man and Socialism in Cuba: The Great Debate* (New York: Antheneum Publishers, 1971).

[24] Reports indicate that in mainland China schoolchildren also celebrate birthdays collectively once a month.

[25] Interview with Consuelo Miranda, Havana, 1969.

[26] For a discussion of these playpens, see the introduction by Urie Bronfenbrenner, in Henry Chauncey, ed., *Soviet Preschool Education, Volume I: Program of Instruction* (New York: Holt, Rinehart and Winston, 1969), p. XII.

[27] Garrity, "Cuba as a Case Study," p. 64.

[28] Miranda interview, 1969.

[29] Similar activities for younger children are also given in círculo planeamientos.

[30] "El Campesino Egoísta," *Simientes*, VII:3 (1969), p. 2.

[31] Miranda interview, 1969.

[32] Consuelo Miranda, "Orientaciones pedagógicas," *Simientes*, IV:26 (1966), pp. 8–11.

[33] Fagen, *Transformation*, p. 11.

[34] Charles Silberman, *Crisis in the Classroom: The Remaking of American Education* (New York: Random House, 1970), p. 9.

[35] David Rosenham, Preface to Henry Chauncey, ed., *Soviet Preschool Education, Vol. II: Teacher's Commentary* (New York: Holt, Rinehart and Winston, 1969), pp. v–vi.

[36] Urie Bronfenbrenner, *Two Worlds of Childhood: U.S. and U.S.S.R.* (New York: Russell Sage Foundation, 1970), p. 158.

[37] Katherine H. Read, *The Nursery School* (Philadelphia: W. B. Saunders Company, 1960).

[38] See Samuel Bowles, "Cuban Education and the Revolutionary Ideology," *Harvard Educational Review*, XLI:4 (Nov. 1971), pp. 472–500. The quotation was taken from an original draft of the article with the permission of the author. It was deleted from the final version.

II. PERSONNEL: THE PARAPROFESSIONAL SOLUTION

[1] Marvin Leiner, "Cuba's Schools, Ten Years Later," *Saturday Review*, Oct. 17, 1970, p. 59.

[2] Richard Jolly, "Education," in Dudley Seers, ed., *Cuba: The Economic and Social Revolution* (Chapel Hill: University of North Carolina Press, 1964), p. 177.

[3] Interview with Dr. Consuelo Miranda, Havana, Aug. 1971.

[4] Ernesto Che Guevara, "Letter to Fidel," in John Gerassi, ed., *Venceremos!: The Speeches and Writings of Ernesto Che Guevara* (New York: The Macmillan Company, 1968), pp. 410–411.

[5] Until 1971 applicants for the training program for asistentes were accepted up to the age of 30.

[6] Miranda interview, Aug. 1971.

[7] Interview with Marta Santander, Havana, Aug. 1971.

[8] From interview with team of psychologists working with the Jardines Infantiles, Havana, 1969.

[9] Interview with Lela Sánchez, Havana, Sept. 1971.

[10] Interview with jardín psychologists, 1969.

[11] *Ibid.*

[12] Nancy Garrity, "Cuba as a Case Study: The Role Played by Education in the Socialization of the New Man" (Ph.D. diss., Tufts University, 1971), p. 15.

[13] Miranda interview, 1969.

[14] Sergio León and Franklin Martínez, "Creación de un instrumento para medir vocación para trabajar con niños menores de cinco años," *Psicología y educación,* July–Dec. 1968, pp. 25–62.

[15] *Ibid.,* p. 38.

[16] Thirty percent of those women who enter the círculo asistente program reportedly fail to live up to the personality requirements set by the leadership.

[17] Miranda interview, 1971.

[18] Miranda interview, Havana, 1969.

[19] *Ibid.*

[20] *Ibid.*

[21] *Ibid.*

[22] David Rosenham, Preface to Henry Chauncey, ed., *Soviet Preschool Education; Teacher's Commentary* (New York: Holt, Rinehart and Winston, 1969), p. XI.

[23] Sánchez interview, 1971.

[24] Santander interview, 1971.

[25] See Merle B. Karnes, R. Reid Zehrbach, and James A. Teska, "A New Professional Role in Early Childhood Education," *Interchange,* II:2 (Ontario: Ontario Institute for Studies in Education, 1971), pp. 80–105.

[26] During 1971, there was much political and educational discussion in the United States of America about increasing day-care education for low-income families. It is interesting to note that a number of the new projected proposals for day-care training recognize the reality of meeting the manpower problem by training non-college-degree staff.

On December 23, 1971, the Director of the Office of Child Development (a division of the U.S. Department of Health, Education and Welfare), Dr. Edward Zigler, announced that a new type of position would be created—a "Child Development Associate." This person would be someone who did not have four years of college but who had had training in concepts of child development. Dr. Zigler stated: "We could say that every day-care teacher needs a bachelor's degree and the supply would never meet the demand. . . . It is very easy for people to insist you have the very best, but then you often wind up with unrealistic demands. If you did this with day care, you would not upgrade quality, you would drive day care underground. With unrealistically high standards, you could make services worse." *New York Times*, December 24, 1971, p. 16.

III. THE SCHOOLS

[1] Bettye M. Caldwell, "A Timid Giant Grows Bolder," *Saturday Review*, Feb. 20, 1971, p. 47.

[2] *Granma*, II:6 (Feb. 5, 1967), p. 3.

[3] *Ibid.*

[4] Nancy Garrity, "Cuba as a Case Study: The Role Played by Education in the Socialization of the New Man" (M.A. thesis, Tufts University, 1971), p. 60.

[5] Clementina Serra, Letter to Marvin Leiner, Sept. 9, 1971.

[6] Mirta Rodríguez Calderón, "Interview with Vilma Espín, President of the FMC, on Occasion of the 13th Anniversary of that Organization," *Granma Weekly Review*, Sept. 2, 1973, p. 2.

[7] Clementina Serra, "Report on the Círculos Infantiles," typewritten (July 13, 1969), p. 5.

[8] *Granma*, II:6 (Feb. 5, 1967), pp. 2–3.

[9] Garrity, "Cuba as a Case Study," p. 22.

[10] Interview with Dr. Consuelo Miranda, Havana, 1969.

[11] John K. Fairbank, "Getting to Know You," *New York Review of Books*, XVIII (Feb. 24, 1972), p. 3.

[12] Garrity, "Cuba as a Case Study."

[13] These schedules for the lactante group (Tables 3–6) were posted in the Raúl Pérez círculo, Havana. A check of círculo schedules in other parts of Cuba indicated that with slight variation, the same basic schedules were in operation. In my visit to the La Máquina círculo, in Oriente, the lactante schedule provided similar time allotments for the various activities. La Máquina had to be reached by jeep or burro because of its location in the Sierra Mountains, in the area known as Gran Tierra. The círculo was opened in September 1967 and has spacious rooms facing a green courtyard garden. The sixty children were serviced by a staff of fifteen people. In 1967, when the círculo opened, the peasants were reluctant to send their children. Now, according to the young director, the círculo is popular with parents, who not only send their preschool children, but offer to help "their círculo."

[14] Departmento de Educación, Dirección Nacional de Círculos Infantiles," Orientaciones Generales Para las Compañeras Asistentes de los Círculos Infantiles: Sala de Lactantes, mimeographed (Havana, Feb. 1969), pp. 2–4.

[15] Santander interview, 1971.

[16] Interview with Dr. Consuelo Miranda, Havana, 1971.

[17] Santander interview, 1971.

[18] Garrity, "Cuba as a Case Study," p. 34.

[19] Peggy Schirmer in Garrity, "Cuba as a Case Study," pp. 67–68.

[20] *Ibid.*, p. 71.

[21] Marvin Leiner, "Cuba's Schools, Ten Years Later," *Saturday Review*, Oct. 17, 1970, p. 60. See also Samuel Bowles, "Cuban Education and the Revolutionary Ideology," *Harvard Educational Review*, XLI:4 (Nov. 1971), pp. 472–500. Bowles analyzes the correspondence between economic and educational objectives and considers the dilemmas in the continuing revolutionary development of Cuban education.

[22] Garrity, "Cuba as a Case Study," p. 69.

[23] Departmento de Educación, "Orientaciones Generales," p. 3.

[24] Garrity, "Cuba as a Case Study," 67, 22.

[25] *Ibid.*, p. 75.

[26] *Ibid.*, p. 70.

[27] *Ibid.*, p. 69.

[28] Tables 8–10 were copied from schedules posted at the Raúl Pérez círculo in Havana.

[29] Garrity, "Cuba as a Case Study," p. 76.

[30] "La adaptación del niño al círulo," *Simientes* VI:48 (1968), p. 8.

[31] J. Pérez Villar, *Etapas del desarrollo y trastornos emocionales en el niño* (Havana: Instituto del Libro, 1967), pp. 85–87.

[32] Interview with Arsenio Carmona, Havana, 1969.

[33] Interview with Consuelo Miranda, Havana, 1969.

[34] Sally Provence, *Guide for the Care of Infants in Groups* (New York: Child Welfare League of America, 1967).

[35] Willis F. Overton, "Piaget's Theory of Intellectual Development and Progressive Education," in James R. Squire, ed., *A New Look at Progressive Education* (Washington: Association for Supervision and Curriculum Development, 1972), pp. 113–114.

[36] J. McVicker Hunt, "The Implications of Changing Ideas on How Children Develop Intellectually," *Children*, May–June, 1964; Martin Deutsch, et al., *The Disadvantaged Child: Selected Papers of Martin Deutsch* (New York: Basic Books, 1967); David Weikert, et al., *The Cognitively Oriented Curriculum: A Framework for Preschool Teachers* (Washington: National Association for the Education of Young Children, 1971); Carl Bereiter and Siegfried Engelmann, *Teaching Disadvantaged Children in the Preschool* (Englewood Cliffs, N.J.: Prentice Hall, 1966). For collections of articles on early childhood developments in the past decade see Joe L. Frost, ed., *Early Childhood Rediscovered* (New York: Holt, Rinehart and Winston, 1968); Willard W. Hartup and Nancy L. Smothergill, eds., *The Young Child: Reviews of Research* (Washington: National Association for the Education of Young Children, 1970); R. K. Parker, et al., *Overview of Cognitive and Language Programs for Three-, Four-, and Five-Year-Old Children* (New York: City University of New York, Center for Advanced Study in Education, 1970); Edith Grotberg, ed., *Critical Issues in Research Related to Disadvantaged Children* (Princeton: Educational Testing Service, 1969); Andrew Effat, ed., "Early Learning," *Interchange*, II:2 (Ontario: The Ontario Institute for Studies in Education, 1971); and Ralph R. Sleeper, ed., "Early

Childhood Education: A Perspective," *Educational Leadership*, XXVIII:8 (May, 1971).

[37] Martin Deutsch, "Facilitating Development in the Pre-School Child: Social and Psychological Perspectives," *Merrill-Palmer Quarterly of Behaviour and Development*, X:3 (July, 1964), p. 258.

[38] Clementina Serra, "Report on the Círculos Infantiles," typewritten (July 13, 1969), pp. 1–41.

[39] Deutsch, "Facilitating Development," pp. 249–263.

[40] Clementina Serra, "Report on the Círculos Infantiles," pp. 18–20.

[41] Interview with Marta Santander, Havana, 1969.

[42] "Nuestros Amigos: Los Guerrilleros: Planeamiento, Semana 6," in *Planeamientos: Semanas 1–8*, mimeographed (Havana: Dirección Nacional de Círculos Infantiles, 1969), pp. 7–12.

[43] Santander interview, 1969.

[44] Santander interview, 1971.

[45] Miranda interview, 1971.

[46] *Ibid.*

[47] *Ibid.*

[48] Burton L. White, "An Analysis of Excellent Early Educational Practices: Preliminary Report," *Interchange*, II:2 (1971), pp. 71–88.

[49] Interview with Lela Sánchez, Havana, 1971.

[50] Jardines Infantiles y MINSAP (Ministerio de Salud Pública), *Orientaciones psicopedagógicas, su niño de cero a cinco años*. For some of the directives, see pp. 152–161.

[51] Interview with Lela Sánchez, Havana, 1971.

[52] Private communication with Ruth Lewis.

[53] *Plan especial de jardines infantiles; bases científicas del plan de jardines infantiles*, mimeographed (Havana, 1968), pp. 1–2.

[54] *Ibid.*, p. 2.

[55] *Ibid.*, p. 8.

[56] Interview with Haydée Salas, Havana, 1969.

[57] Ruth Lewis, "Attitudes of Parents Towards the Jardín Experience at a Jardín Infantil in Havana," unpublished (private communication with Ruth Lewis).

[58] Sánchez interview, 1971.

[59] D. E. M. Gardner, *Education Under Eight* (London: Methuen & Co., Ltd., 1949), p. 18.

[60] Interview with psychologists working with the Jardines Infantiles, Havana, 1969.

[61] Sánchez interview, 1971.

[62] Interview with jardín psychologists, 1969.

[63] *Ibid.*

[64] *Ibid.*

[65] Salas interview, 1969.

[66] *Plan especial de jardines.*

[67] See J. Piaget and B. Inhelder, *The Psychology of the Child* (New York: Basic Books, 1969); J. Flavell, *The Developmental Psychology of Jean Piaget* (Princeton: D. Van Nostrand, 1963); J. L. Phillips, *The Origins of Intellect: Piaget's Theory* (San Francisco: W. H. Freeman and Company, 1969); and Carole Hornstead, "The Developmental Theory of Jean Piaget," in Joe L. Frost, ed., *Early Childhood Rediscovered* (New York: Holt, Rinehart and Winston, 1968).

[68] Erik H. Erikson, *Childhood and Society*, rev. ed. (New York: Norton, 1963).

[69] Consuelo Miranda, "Orientaciones pedagógicas," *Simientes*, IV:32 (1966), p. 25.

[70] Sánchez interview, 1971.

[71] Jacob Gerwirtz, "The Role of Stimulation in Models for Child Development," in Laura Dittman, ed. *Early Child Care: New Perspectives* (New York: Atherton Press, 1968); see also Gerwirtz, "On Designing the Functional Environment of the Child to Facilitate Behavioural Development," in the same volume.

[72] Sánchez interview, 1971.

[73] Private communication with Ruth Lewis.

[74] *Plan especial de jardínes infantiles*, p. 3.

IV. NUTRITION AND HEALTH CARE

[1] See Herbert G. Birch and Joan Dye Gussow, *Disadvantaged Children: Health, Nutrition and School Failure* (New York: Harcourt, Brace and World, 1970); Sylvia Sunderlin, *Nutrition and*

Intellectual Growth in Children (Washington: Association for Childhood Educational International, 1969); Edwin H. Grutberg, "Nutrition and Learning," in William Polder, ed., *Abstracts II: 1970 Annual Meeting Symposia, American Educational Research Association* (Washington: American Educational Research Association, 1970); and J. Cravioto, "Malnutrition and Behavioral Development in the Preschool Child," in *Preschool Child Malnutrition: Primary Deterrent to Human Progress; An International Conference on Prevention of Malnutrition in the Preschool Child,* National Academy of Sciences–National Research Council Publication No. 1282 (Washington, 1966).

2 Ira J. Gordon, *On Early Learning: The Modifiability of Human Potential* (Washington: Association for Supervision and Curriculum Development, 1971), p. 26.

3 *Ibid.*, p. 20; also see Merle B. Karnes, R. Reid Zehrbach, and James A. Teska, "A New Professional Role in Early Childhood Education," *Interchange,* II:2 (1971), p. 89.

4 *Ibid.*, p. 4; also see J. Cravioto, Elsa R. Delicardie, and H. G. Birch, "Nutrition, Growth and Neurointegrative Development: an Experimental and Ecologic Study," *Pediatrics,* XXXVIII:2, Part II, Suppl. (1966), pp. 319–372.

5 Birch and Gussow, *Disadvantaged Children,* p. 268.

6 Clementina Serra, "Report on the Círculos Infantiles," typewritten (July 13, 1969), p. 13.

7 Marta Santander and Consuelo Miranda, "Círculos Infantiles: la educación en la edad temprana," in *Seminario interdisciplinario de educación* permanente, mimeographed (Havana, 1970), pp. 3–4.

8 *Ibid.*, p. 5.

9 *Granma,* Jan. 22, 1967, p. 3.

10 In Cuba, school children of all ages wear uniforms. Even círculo children as young as two and three years of age are given special attire.

Asistentes wear blue uniforms with white kerchiefs and the kitchen staff wear white attire and white kerchiefs. Those teachers educated at the Makarenko Institute wear an altogether special uniform to distinguish them from the others.

The argument over uniforms is an old one. Should school children be required to wear special clothing or should they be permitted to wear whatever they have at home? Those who are in favor of uniforms for school children argue that clothes should not be an area of competition among children. One child (because of his financial position or because of this parent's indulgence) should not be permitted to show off to his schoolmates. Conversely, children should not be penalized because of economic circumstances. A recent private communication from Cuba indicates that changes are being effected in day-care uniforms. In some centers children now wear uniforms bearing individualized symbols for each child. For example, one child may have an elephant on his shirt as well as on all other items of apparel, while another may have a flower, etc.

[11] Interview with Dr. Consuelo Miranda, Havana, 1969.

[12] Departmento de Salud, "El baño de los niños en el círculo infantil," *Simientes*, IX:10 (1971), pp. 10–11.

[13] Interview with Lela Sánchez, 1971.

[14] Consuelo Miranda, "Orientaciones pedagógicas," *Simientes*, IV:26 (1966), p. 8.

[15] *Planeamientos: Semanas 1–8*, (Havana: Dirección Nacional de Círculos Infantiles, 1969).

[16] Nancy Garrity, "Cuba as a Case Study: The Role Played by Education in the Socialization of the New Man" (M.A. thesis, Tufts University, 1971), p. 72.

[17] Miranda interview, 1971.

[18] Erik H. Erikson, *Childhood and Society*, rev. ed. (New York: Norton, 1963).

[19] Myron Winick, "Nutrition and Intellectual Development in Children," in Sylvia Sunderlin, ed., *Nutrition and Intellectual Growth*, p. 27.

[20] Ministerio de Salud Pública, *Manual de dietética para círculos infantiles*, mimeographed (Havana, 1963).

[21] Roslyn B. Alfin-Slater, Head of the Division of Environmental and Nutritional Sciences of the School of Public Health at the University of California at Los Angeles, warns that caloric excesses, too, can lead to difficulties. It is now believed that fat children

have extra adipose tissue cells which never disappear; a fat child becomes a fat adult at the slightest provocation.

[22] *Manual de dietética*, pp. 25–34, 11–15.

[23] Garrity, "Cuba as a Case Study," p. 75.

[24] Peggy Schirmer, personal communication, also cited in *ibid.*, p. 64.

[25] Departmento de Educación, Dirección Nacional de Círculos Infantiles, "Curso de Superación para las Compañeras Asistentes de los Círculos Infantiles: Lineamientos de un Plan de Trabajo con el Grupo de los Parvulitos," mimeographed (Havana, April, 1969), pp. 1–6.

[26] Ministerio de Salud Pública, *Reglamento de salud pública para los círculos infantiles* (Havana: Ministerio de Salud Pública, 1969), pp. 1–5.

V. THE FAMILY AND THE COMMUNITY

[1] Maurice Zeitlin, "Cuba—Revolution Without a Blueprint," *Transaction*, VI:6 (April 1969), p. 38.

[2] Friedrich Engels, "On the Origins of the Family, Private Property, and the State," in Karl Marx and Friedrich Engels, *Selected Works*, II (Moscow: Foreign Languages Publishing House, 1962).

[3] Raymond Leslie Buell, et al., *The Problems of the New Cuba: Report of the Commission on Cuban Affairs* (New York: Foreign Policy Association, 1935), pp. 68–69.

[4] A. S. Makarenko, *The Collective Family: A Handbook for Parents* (New York: Doubleday, 1967), p. xi. The Russian edition was published in the Soviet Union in 1937. The translation in the Doubleday edition was published as a *Book for Parents* by the Foreign Languages Publishing House, Moscow.

[5] Urie Bronfenbrenner, "Makarenko and the Collective Family," in Makarenko, *Collective Family*, p. XI.

[6] Interview with Dr. Consuelo Miranda, Havana, 1969. While Cubans feel that boarding schools are not appropriate for early childhood programs, they encourage boarding schools at the ju-

nior high and senior high levels. See Marvin Leiner, *The Integration of Formal and Non-Formal Rural Education in Cuba: The Countryside Programs.* (A Case Study prepared for UNICEF: in preparation).

[7] Miranda interview, 1969.

[8] *Ibid.*

[9] Ira J. Gordon, *On Early Learning: The Modifiability of Human Potential* (Washington: Association for Supervision and Curriculum Development, 1971), p. 11.

[10] Marta Santander and Consuelo Miranda, "Círculos infantiles: la educación en la edad temprana," in *Seminario interdisciplinario de educación permanente,* mimeographed (Havana, 1970), p. 3.

[11] Sergio León and Franklin Martínez, "Creación de un instrumento para medir vocación para trabajar con niños menores de cinco años," *Psicología y educación,* July–Dec. 1968, pp. 26–27.

[12] Santander and Miranda, "Círculos Infantiles," p. 2.

[13] Fidel Castro, speech presented at the closing session of the national meeting of school monitors, *Granma Weekly Review,* Sept. 25, 1966, p. 4.

[14] Santander and Miranda, "Círculos Infantiles," p. 11.

[15] *Ibid.*

[16] Hron, Fantišek, "¿Pertenecen los niños a la familia o a la escuela?" *Simientes,* III:19 (1965), pp. 14–15.

[17] Consuelo Miranda, "Orientaciones pedagógicas," *Simientes,* IV:27 (1966), pp. 11–12.

[18] Chaim Ginott, *Between Parent and Child* (New York: Macmillan, 1965).

[19] Departamento de Capacitación y Superación del Personal (DINCI), "Educación de padres," *Simientes,* IX:10 (1971), p. 6.

[20] Merle B. Karnes, R. Reid Zehrbach, and James A. Teska, "A New Professional Role in Early Childhood Education," *Interchange,* II:2 (Ontario: Ontario Institute for Studies in Education, 1971), p. 89.

[21] Bronfenbrenner, "Makarenko," p. 160.

[22] Jardines Infantiles y MINSAP (Ministerio de Salud Publica), *Orientaciones psicopedagógicas, su niño de cero a cinco años.* This is the source for all subsequent references to the cards.

[23] Fidel Castro, address delivered on March 13, 1968, on the eleventh anniversary of the attack on the Presidential Palace, in Martin Kenner and James Petras, eds., *Fidel Castro Speaks* (New York: Grove Press, 1969), p. 278.

[24] Interview with Miguel Formosa, administrator of a refrigerator plant, Havana, 1969.

[25] *Ibid.*

VI. CUBAN DAY CARE REVISITED

[1] "Official Proclamation Creating the Children's Institute," in *Granma*, June 6, 1971, p. 4.

[2] Interview with Dr. Daniel Alonso, Havana, 1971.

[3] Interview with Vilma Espín, Havana, 1971.

[4] Alonso interview, 1971.

[5] *Ibid.*

[6] *Ibid.*

[7] Article 2, "Official Proclamation." According to the proclamation, the "other groups" include the *hogares cunas* and *hogares infantiles*. These are centers for children who need special care, e.g., orphans with no immediate family to take care of them.

[8] Alonso interview, 1971.

[9] *Ibid.*

[10] Interview with Dr. Consuelo Miranda, Havana, 1971.

[11] Alonso interview, 1971.

[12] Interview with staff member at jardín infantil, Havana, 1971.

[13] Interview with Lela Sánchez, Havana, 1971.

[14] *Ibid.*

[15] Lillian Weber, *The English Infant School and Informal Education* (Englewood Cliffs, N.J.: Prentice Hall, 1971), pp. 33–34.

[16] Espín interview, 1971.

[17] UNESCO, *XXXIII International Conference on Public Instruction, OIE–UNESCO, September 15–23, 1971; Report of Cuba; Organization of Education, 1970–71* (UN Doc. OIE/Q/70/3), p. 14.

[18] Conversation with factory worker at escuela en el campo, Havana, 1971.

[19] UNESCO, *International Conference*, p. 13.

[20] *Ibid.*, p. 24.

[21] *Ibid.*, pp. 25, 30, 32–33.

[22] *Ibid.*, p. 32.

[23] Conversation with member of UNEAC, the Cuban Union of Writers and Artists, 1971.

[24] UNESCO, *International Conference*, pp. 30–31.

[25] *Ibid.*, p. 30.

[26] Interview with Dr. Max Figueroa Araujo, Havana, 1971.

[27] Richard R. Fagen, *The Transformation of Political Culture in Cuba* (Stanford: Stanford University Press, 1969), p. 35.

[28] Fidel Castro, *Revolución*, Sept. 7, 1961, p. 6, as quoted in Fagen, p. 35.

[29] *Early Childhood Development: Alternatives for Program Implementation in the States. A Report of the Education Commission of the States Task Force on Early Childhood Education* (Denver: Education Commission of the States, 1971), p. 81.

[30] Interview with Marta Santander, 1971.